How Strong Is Your Firm's Competitive Advantage?

How Strong Is Your Firm's Competitive Advantage?

Second Edition

Daniel Marburger

 BUSINESS EXPERT PRESS

How Strong Is Your Firm's Competitive Advantage?, Second Edition

First published in 2012 by
Business Expert Press, LLC
222 East 46th Street, New York, NY 10017
www.businessexpertpress.com

ISBN-13: 978-1-63157-367-5 (paperback)
ISBN-13: 978-1-63157-368-2 (e-book)

Business Expert Press Economics Collection

Collection ISSN: 2163-761X (print)
Collection ISSN: 2163-7628 (electronic)

Cover and interior design by Exeter Premedia Services Private Ltd., Chennai, India

First edition: 2012
Second edition: 2016

10 9 8 7 6 5 4 3 2 1

Printed in the United States of America

Abstract

Perhaps the most confounding characteristic of the competitive market-place is that everyone wants a piece of the action. If a firm successfully enters a new market, creates a new product, or designs new innovations for an existing product, it's just a matter of time before competitors follow suit. And the influx of competition inevitably places downward pressure on both price and profitability. But the speed at which competitors invade one's market is not the same in all industries; some are more resistant to the forces of competition than others. In 1979, Harvard economist Michael Porter theorized his Five Forces Model (updated in 2008). The Five Forces Model identifies the characteristics that can help insulate a firm from competitive forces. For the firm that seeks to put together a business plan, or for the firm that is considering opportunities for diversification, an understanding of the Five Forces Model is essential.

Keywords

Porter's Five Forces, bargaining power, market power, market barriers, product differentiation, product substitution, switching costs

Contents

List of Firms/Products

Chapter 3

1. Borders Group and Kobo Inc.
2. Barnes & Noble and Amazon
3. Blockbuster
4. Redbox
5. Toyota and Honda
6. Yahoo! and Google
7. Apple iTunes
8. Nielsen
9. Rhapsody
10. Kia
11. Trek
12. Hyundai
13. Motorola, Nokia, and BellSouth—IBM
14. Samsung
15. Ericsson
16. Siemens
17. Walmart
18. Circuit City and Best Buy
19. Target
20. AT&T
21. Dell Computers
22. Billboard
23. Pepsi
24. Media Monkey
25. Sharepod
26. Tylenol
27. Kmart
28. Microsoft
29. Verizon
30. Spotify

4. McMenamins

5. Ford, General Motors, and Chrysler

6. Toyota, Nissan, and Honda

7. Shell

8. BP

Chapter 6

1. Kenmore

2. Whirlpool Corporation and General Electric

3. Sears and Kmart

4. Northrop Grumman

5. Department of Defense

6. QWERTY and Dvorak keyboards

7. Virgin Records

8. BMW Group

9. Dollar General

10. DuPont and STAINMASTER

11. brands Post

12. General Mills

13. Kellogg

14. Quaker Oats

Chapter 7

1. Enron

2. American International Group, Inc.

3. Samsung and Sharp

4. Visa and MasterCard

5. McDonald's and Subway

6. Hilton—American Express Card

PART I

If You Could Choose Any Price, What Would It Be? Fundamentals for the Single Price Firm

CHAPTER 1

Economics and the Business Manager

What Is Economics All About?

Mention the word *economist* and one conjures up a vision of an academic who scours over macroeconomic data and utilizes sophisticated statistical techniques to make forecasts. Indeed, that's what many economists do. But some people may be surprised to learn that economics is a social science, not a business science. Like psychology, sociology, anthropology, and the other social sciences, economics studies human behavior. It includes consumer behavior, firm behavior, and the behavior of markets.

In its simplest form, economics is a study of how human beings behave when they cannot be in two places at the same time. If a person takes a job that requires extensive travel, the income and opportunities for advancement come at the expense of spending time at home. The idea that we cannot have all the things we want is called *scarcity*, and it plays a role in every decision we make; not just financial decisions, but non-financial ones as well. Do you want to stay up late to watch the ball game on TV if it means you won't get a full night's sleep? Do you want to read the financial pages on the Internet or watch your son pitch in the Little League game? Scarcity forces us to lay out our opportunities, prioritize our activities, and choose accordingly.

Consumers do the same with their incomes. They cannot spend the same money twice, so scarcity (in the form of a finite income) forces them to determine what they can afford, prioritize the possibilities, and decide what to purchase and what to do without. The latter point, *what to do without,* is relevant to both spending decisions and the uses of one's time. As long as you cannot be in two places at once, whatever you choose implies the alternatives you must forego. Likewise, because you cannot spend the same money twice, each purchase decision you make implies those you cannot make. Economists refer to this as *opportunity cost*. In understanding human behavior, most economists will acknowledge that opportunity cost is the most critical concept in decision making.

Let's begin with a simple example of the role of opportunity cost in business: Negotiating the price of a new car. Most consumers dread negotiating with a salesperson. They assume the salesperson has superior information and will take advantage of them. In fact, the salesperson and customer are negotiating to find a mutually beneficial price; the final act of negotiating is more an act of cooperation than confrontation.

When a consumer decides to purchase a new car, he recognizes that monthly car payments supplant other goods and services he may want to buy. Moreover, the better the car, the higher the price, and the greater the opportunity cost. Opportunity cost helps him determine how much he is willing to spend on the car and what type of vehicles fall within that price range. Once he decides on a vehicle, it's time to sit down with the salesperson and negotiate. The critical element of negotiating is recognizing that both the buyer and seller have alternatives. The seller doesn't have to sell to you. But if the salesperson sells the car to you, he cannot sell it to someone else. The opportunity cost of selling the car to you is the foregone profit he would earn by selling the car to someone else. This represents the lowest price he will accept in a deal. As a prospective buyer, you can go elsewhere. If you buy from this dealer, you will not buy the car from another dealer. Thus, your opportunity cost of buying from this dealer is the price you could likely obtain from a competing dealer. This represents the maximum price you would ever pay to this dealer.

Assume you've staked out the inventories at competing dealerships, determined your willingness to trade away options for a lower price, and researched the dealer cost and average regional sales prices through the Internet. You now have a good idea of the opportunity cost of buying from this dealer. This represents the maximum you would be willing to pay this dealer for the car. The dealer's costs and the price he expects to get from other prospective buyers represent his opportunity cost of selling it to you, and it serves as his minimum price. The price that drives the deal necessarily lies between the opportunity costs of the buyer and seller, and will be mutually beneficial.

Let's review the last point again, as it will prove to be the crucial point in understanding the marketplace. *All transactions between a buyer and a seller are mutually beneficial.* If either party believed it would be worse off by making the transaction, no transaction would take place. Thus, to make a profit, your firm must make an offer that's at least as attractive to the consumer as the available alternatives. In essence, the only way to maximize profits is to *attract* the consumer's money; to offer a product and price that's at least as desirable as those he would forego if he buys from your firm.

What Does Economics Have to Offer to the Business Manager?

Economics studies how individuals deal with scarcity. The theory of the firm is based on the notion that firms seek to maximize profits but must deal with constraints that inhibit their profitability. The constraints incorporate the opportunity costs of those with whom you wish to do business. The most obvious constraint that confronts a firm is the cost of production. Without production, the firm has nothing to sell. A firm requires workers to produce goods. They expect to be compensated for their time and effort. Clearly, higher salaries for the employees mean less profit for the firm. How much, at a minimum, must you pay them? The wage needed to attract labor is driven by opportunity cost. If an individual works for you, he cannot work for someone else. Hence, if you want to hire a worker, you must offer a salary that's at least as good as what he can get from another employer. The salary does not necessarily have to be identical to what competing employers offer. If your workplace is especially unpleasant or dangerous, you may have to pay a premium to lure the individual to your firm. At the opposite extreme, if your work environment is unusually pleasant or offers desirable perks, you may not have to match competing salaries to attract a workforce. The salient point is that your firm's wages are going to be driven by the opportunity cost of the employees you seek to hire.

The same is true for the suppliers of your raw materials. Any item they sell to you cannot be sold to someone else. If you want their business, you must offer a price that's at least as attractive as what they can get from another firm. Note that when it comes to hiring workers or buying materials from prospective suppliers, the opportunity cost of doing business with you drives the wages and prices you must pay.

Beyond the cost of production, the firm's actions are constrained by the opportunity cost of the consumers. From their perspective, the price implies foregone goods and services from other firms. Thus, when consumers see your price, their first instinct is to determine whether they can buy the identical product at a lower price elsewhere. As a result, the more substitutable the good, the less flexibility you have in setting a price.

Suppose your good has no identical substitutes. You may have the only BMW dealership within 100 miles of town. Does that give you market power to set a price of your own choosing? Not really. The consumers don't have to buy a BMW; they can buy another make of car. As the only BMW dealer in town, you'll have more flexibility in setting a price than if there were several BMW dealers in the region, but as long as consumers can find *close* substitutes, the opportunity cost of purchasing from you will influence the price you can charge.

But what if you have no competitors of any kind? To begin with, it's difficult to imagine many circumstances in which *no* substitutes exist. If you owned every car dealership in town, the consumers may deal with out-of-town dealers. If you owned every dealership in the world, consumers might consider buying a bicycle. The price-setting power for the firm increases as the ability to substitute becomes more distant. But the opportunity cost of the consumer still affects the price even if no viable substitute exists. Even without substitutes, the customer doesn't *have* to buy your product. He can choose simply to do without. Thus, even when no apparent substitutes exist, the opportunity cost of the buyer creates boundaries for the price.

It should be obvious that there are innumerable obstacles that can get in the way of profitability, and economists dedicate themselves to studying how profit-seeking firms deal with these constraints. And that's what economics has to offer the business manager. Managers have to deal with the threat of competition, legal constraints, changing consumer tastes, a complex and evolving labor force, and a myriad of other obstacles. The essence of economics is to determine how to deal with the forces of nature that get in the way of the firm's goals.

But what does economics, or, more specifically, managerial economics, have to offer that cannot be found in other business disciplines? Managerial economics should not be viewed as a substitute for other business disciplines. Rather, it serves as the theoretical foundation for the other disciplines. Whereas other business disciplines may elaborate on a set of strategies available to the business manager, a managerial economist can explain the conditions under which they will or will not succeed.

How Does This Text Differ from Other Managerial Economics Textbooks?

Now there's a good question! Before I pursued a PhD in economics, I had an MBA degree and several years of experience with a Fortune 500 company. When I completed the doctorate and began my academic career, I spent many years teaching managerial economics to my MBA students and became quite familiar with the array of textbooks. Along the way, a family member enrolled in an MBA program, and I had a chance to refamiliarize myself with the standard MBA coursework. I began to realize how useful the other courses were, but how useless the managerial economics textbooks were. Not that economics didn't have anything to offer the business manager; rather, most managerial economics textbooks sidestepped issues that business managers would deem useful, and devoted significant space to topics that were far too abstract or esoteric for the manager to use. Indeed, in a survey of over 100 business programs accredited by the Association to Advance Collegiate Schools of Business (AACSB), 54 percent of the respondents described the economics courses required in their MBA programs as either "unpopular" or "very unpopular." The most common reasons for their lack of popularity were that the economics courses were "too theoretical" (30 percent), "too difficult" (23 percent), and "too quantitative" (21 percent).[1]

None of these surprised me. Most managerial economics textbooks devote an inordinate amount of space to elements of theory, which, although useful to economics as a social science, are of minimal use to the practicing business manager. Virtually all managerial economics texts, for example, demonstrate that if a firm wishes to maximize production subject to a budget, it will allocate its resources such that the marginal rate of technical substitution is equal to the ratio of input prices. Confused? Would it help if I drew a graph and showed that production would be maximized where the isoquant is tangent to the ratio of the price of labor relative to the price of capital? I don't think so. I've yet to hear someone from the business community say to me "Boy, I've been sitting on these isoquants all these years, and I never knew what to do with them until I took a course in managerial economics."

The criticism that managerial economics is too quantitative also sounds true. There's nothing wrong with quantitative tools. Indeed, MBA programs teach a great number of tools that can help the business manager make better decisions. I teach statistical tools in my managerial economics class that I think will be very helpful to managers. But what's the point in teaching quantitative skills that business managers will never use? Most managerial economics texts place special emphasis on using algebra and differential calculus to make pricing and output decisions. Curiously, textbooks in the other business disciplines fail to include the use of algebraic equations and calculus to make decisions; in fact, many specifically advise against attempting to do so. To that end, it seems rather illogical to devote time and space to quantitative skills that do not translate particularly well to the real world of the business manager.[2]

The purpose of my contributions to the economics series for Business Expert Press is simple: To bring microeconomic theory into the world of a business manager rather than the other way around. If an element of theory has no practical application, there is no reason to discuss it. Further, if an economic concept does have practical value, it is incumbent upon me to repackage it to suit the manager. In short, my intent is to expound on microeconomic theory that can be taken back to the office and put into use.

Is it necessary for a manager to have a background in economics to read this book? The answer is *no*. My objective is to help managers make better decisions, not to preach to economic majors. I assume that many readers may have had a course or two in microeconomics, and some of the more basic concepts may already be familiar to them. But I've written this textbook under the assumption that some readers may never have had an economics course before. For them, it will be necessary for me to start from scratch. Of course, there may be more than a few readers who have had an economics course in their distant past (like during the dark ages) but have long forgotten what they'd been taught, and may welcome a quick primer on the more basic concepts.

CHAPTER 2

The Shareholders Want Their Profits, and They Want Them Now

Short-Run Profit Maximization for the Firm

Consumer Theory and Demand

Economists assume that the goal of a firm is to maximize profits. Although society frequently scorns firms for their pursuit of money, economists recognize that profits are a motivating factor to produce the goods that consumers want, to find ways to produce efficiently, to develop product attributes that appeal to consumers, and to price competitively. Consumers don't have to buy from your firm. From the consumers' point of view, the price they pay for your good represents opportunity cost: it implies all of the goods and services they must forego if they buy from you. To maximize profits, the firm must *attract* the consumers' money.

To identify the strength of a firm's competitive advantage, we must first understand consumer demand. *Demand* refers to the quantities of a good or service that buyers are willing and able to buy at each price. Suppose you are going to the ball game and have a few dollars to spend on concessions. Assume a hot dog costs $1, as does a Coke. At a break in the game, you decide to visit the concessions stand. Because both goods cost $1, you will purchase the good that gives you more satisfaction. Economists use the word *utility* to refer to satisfaction. *Marginal utility* refers to the satisfaction the individual obtains from one more unit of the good. If you decide to buy the hot dog, we can infer that the marginal utility of the first hot dog ($MU_{HD}{}^1$) gives you more satisfaction than that of the first Coke ($MU_C{}^1$). Later in the game, you return to the concessions stand. This time, you buy the Coke. It must be true that the marginal utility from the first Coke ($MU_C{}^1$) (i.e., additional satisfaction) exceeds the marginal utility from the second hot dog ($MU_{HD}{}^2$).

Your buying habits establish the framework that describes consumer demand. You preferred the first hot dog to the first Coke, but you would rather have your first Coke than your second hot dog.

Let's review your preferences:

1. $MU_{HD}{}^1 > MU_C{}^1$ (the first hot dog is preferred to the first Coke).
2. $MU_C{}^1 > MU_{HD}{}^2$ (the first Coke is preferred to the second hot dog).

If the first hot dog is preferred to the first Coke, but the first Coke is preferred to the second hot dog, then it also follows that the first hot dog is preferred to the second hot dog, or

3. $MU_{HD}{}^1 > MU_{HD}{}^2$ (the first hot dog is preferred to the second hot dog).

Economists refer to this as the *law of diminishing marginal utility*. It suggests that the additional satisfaction derived from each additional unit diminishes as more units are consumed. If this were not true, you would go to the game and spend all of your money on hot dogs. Because consumers spread their money around to buy a wide array of products, we can infer that the law of diminishing marginal utility plays a role in virtually all purchase decisions.

If each unit provides the buyer with less additional satisfaction, it must also be true that the buyer is willing to spend less on each additional unit. Suppose you are willing to spend up to $1.25 for the first hot dog, $0.75 for the second hot dog, and $0.50 for the third hot dog. Collectively, we can derive the *law of demand*. If the price of hot dogs is $1.25, then you would only be willing to buy one because the other hot dogs do not provide sufficient satisfaction to justify the price. If the price of hot dogs fell to $0.75, you would be willing to buy two hot dogs. The

Table 2.1 *Individual demand schedule*

Quantity	Willing to spend
1	$1.25
2	$0.75
3	$0.50

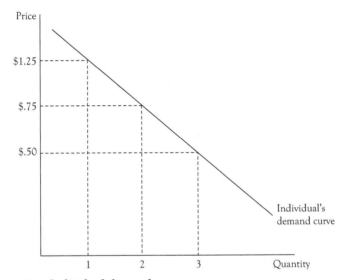

Figure 2.1 *Individual demand curve*

second hot dog now justifies the expenditure, but the third one does not. The law of demand states that as the price of a good rises, the quantity demanded decreases and vice versa. Your demand for hot dogs appears in Table 2.1 and is expressed graphically in Figure 2.1.

The demand for a good or service produced by an individual firm is simply the sum of the quantities demanded by each consumer. An example appears in Table 2.2, with the corresponding firm demand curve illustrated in Figure 2.2. The firm's demand indicates the quantities of a good or services that buyers are willing and able to buy at each price.

There is one critical element of the firm's demand curve that cannot be sidestepped. The concession stand example was used because consumers have limited choice options. If a consumer wants a hot dog, he cannot choose from competing brands. Most stadiums do not permit

Table 2.2 Firm demand schedule

| Price | Quantity demanded by | | | |
	Amber	Bruce	Casey	Total firm demand
$1.25	0	1	1	2
$0.75	1	2	1	4
$0.50	2	2	2	6

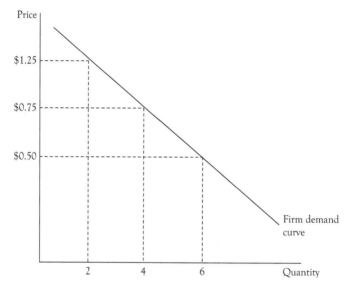

Figure 2.2 Firm demand curve

the buyer to enter with food purchased outside the stadium. Therefore, if the consumer wants to eat or drink during the game, he must buy from the concession stand. This strengthens the firm's competitive position considerably. However, even these constraints do not afford unbridled market power because the consumer can choose not to purchase from the concession stand at all. He might decide that he would rather spend his money on goods that can be purchased after the game. Therefore, we want our definition of firm demand to implicitly acknowledge that Amber, Bruce, and Casey can spend their money before or after the game, and that this is embedded in their individual demands in Table 2.2.

The Law of Demand and Marginal Revenue

The law of demand asserts that as the price of the good rises, the quantity demanded by consumers falls. Conversely, the law also states that the more units the firm wishes to sell, the lower the price it must charge.

Marginal revenue is the additional revenue generated from the additional output. It is an important piece of the puzzle in terms of production decisions. When determining whether to increase production, the firm wants to know how much additional revenue will be generated. Such decisions cannot be made in a vacuum. The firm cannot assume that the additional production can be sold at the existing price. Instead, the quantity it sells is going to be dictated by the law of demand.

At first glance, one might assume that the marginal revenue generated by a unit of output is equal to its price. But this is not the case. To illustrate, examine the information given in Table 2.2. If the firm charges $1.25, it can sell two hot dogs. If it lowers the price to $0.75, it can sell four hot dogs. Is the marginal revenue from the two additional hot dogs equal to $1.50 ($0.75 × two hot dogs)?

Let's examine this decision closely. According to Table 2.2, it can sell two hot dogs at a price of $1.25. This would generate revenues totaling $2.50. If it lowers the price to $0.75, the firm could sell four hot dogs. Note that the firm's revenue at this price would be $3. Thus, increasing unit sales from two hot dogs to four hot dogs raised revenue by $0.50. Why only $0.50? Why not $1.50?

If we break the decision down into two parts, we can see what happened. On the one hand, the firm sold two additional hot dogs at a price of $0.75 each. Economists refer to the $1.50 generated by the two hot dogs as the *output effect*. But this is only half the story. When the firm decided to sell four hot dogs, it lowered the price to $0.75 on all four hot dogs, not just the last two. Therefore, in addition to selling two additional hot dogs for $0.75 each, the firm lowered the price on the first two hot dogs from $1.25 to $0.75. In other words, the firm has to forego $1 ($0.50 on each of the first two hot dogs) in order to sell four hot dogs. The $0.50 price reduction on the first two hot dogs is called the *price effect*. The marginal revenue is the sum of the output and price effects.

Table 2.3 Firm demand and marginal revenue

Price	Firm demand	Total revenue	Marginal revenue
$1.25	2	$2.50	$2.50
$0.75	4	$3	$0.50
$0.50	6	$3	$0

In this case, by increasing unit sales from two hot dogs to four hot dogs, the firm's revenue increased by the sum of the output ($1.50) and price effects (–$1), or by $0.50.

The implications of the law of demand on marginal revenue cannot be understated. It is too convenient to assume that marginal revenue consists only of output effects: that additional production can be sold at the prevailing price. But the law of demand states that most production increases necessitate lowering the price. For this reason, it is imperative that firms consider potential price effects when making production decisions.

To illustrate its importance, consider Table 2.3. This summarizes the same firm demand information contained in Table 2.2. As noted earlier, if the firm wants to increase the sale of hot dogs from two to four, it must drop the price from $1.25 to $0.75. This causes revenues to increase by $0.50. Now consider the implications from increasing unit sales from four to six. As the table indicates, if the firm wants to sell six hot dogs, it must lower its price from $0.75 to $0.50. Note that this decision does not result in any additional revenue. By breaking this down, we know that the output effect is the revenue generated by the fifth and sixth hot dogs. As each hot dog will be sold for $0.50, the output effect is $1. But this is completely offset by the price effect. If the firm wishes to sell six hot dogs, it must lower the price to $0.50 for all six hot dogs, not just the last two. This causes the revenue generated from the first four hot dogs to decrease by $1 ($0.25 price reduction on four hot dogs). Even though the firm sold two additional hot dogs, its revenue did not change.

This is illustrated graphically in Figure 2.3. The demand curve shows the number of hot dogs that can be sold at each price. Note that the marginal revenue curve lies beneath the demand curve. Whereas the demand curve indicates that four hot dogs can be sold at a price of $0.75, the marginal revenue curve shows that increasing unit sales from two to

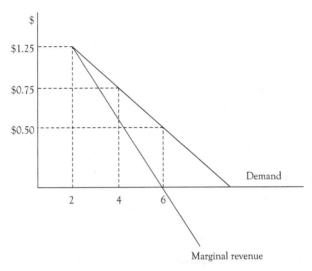

Figure 2.3 The demand curve and marginal revenue

four generates additional revenue equal to $0.50, which is the sum of the output and price effects.

Production Costs

Now that we've covered the demand implications of production and pricing decisions, we must consider the cost side. Economists and accountants define *fixed costs* and *variable costs*. Fixed costs are the expenses that do not vary with production. These would include rent, management salaries, insurance, fixed overhead, and so forth.[1] Variable costs are the expenses that vary with output. These would include direct labor, direct materials, and variable overhead.

Economists define *marginal cost* as the additional costs generated by an increase in production. Because fixed costs do not vary with production, the marginal cost associated with an increase in output must, by definition, be variable.

To illustrate the relationship between production and costs, assume that a group of three teenagers is considering raising money by devoting a Saturday afternoon to washing cars. Because the money is primarily to help fund a high school trip, each participant will only get paid $3 for

Table 2.4 The relationship between cars and costs

Quantity per hour	Fixed cost	Variable cost	Total cost	Marginal cost	Average total cost
0	$10	$0	$10	—	
1	$10	$3	$13	$3	$13
2	$10	$5	$15	$2	$7.50
3	$10	$7.50	$17.50	$2.50	$5.83
4	$10	$11	$21	$3.50	$5.25
5	$10	$16	$26	$5	$5.20
6	$10	$23	$33	$7	$5.50
7	$10	$32	$42	$9	$6

the hour (with fractional payments for fractional hours), and only those who are actively washing cars will get paid. They bought the car-washing liquid and sponges at a cost of $10. The parents allow them to use the hose for free, so they incur no cost from rinsing each vehicle.

Table 2.4 shows the costs associated with the number of cars washed each hour. Note that because the washing liquid and sponges were purchased in advance, they serve as fixed costs and do not vary with the number of cars washed. If no cars are washed, the total cost consists only of the $10 spent on liquid and sponges.

According to Table 2.4, if one car is washed in the hour, the variable cost will be equal to $3. Implicitly, this suggests that one teenager will be called upon to wash the car. Note what happens when the number of washed cars rises from one to two. If one teenager gets paid $3 to wash one car, then the variable cost associated with washing two cars would logically be $6. Why does the variable cost only rise to $5?

Indeed, if the teens arranged the work in such a way that each car would be washed by one person, doubling the number of cars washed would double the variable costs. But if the objective of the teenagers is to raise money for the fundraiser, we can assume they will wash the cars as efficiently as possible. Although they have the option of having one teenager wash each car, they will probably realize that if they divvy up the labor responsibilities (i.e., one person washes and the other rinses, or one person washes the front, one the rear, and one rinses), they could complete each car faster.[2] This is implied in Table 2.4. The variable cost associated with washing one car per hour is $3. If two cars are washed each hour, the variable costs rise, but only to $5. Thus, it is more efficient to wash two cars per hour (the variable cost is $2.50 per car) than one car per hour ($3 per car). We can see the increase in efficiency more clearly by examining the marginal cost associated with each of the first two cars. The additional cost associated with washing the first car is $3, whereas the marginal cost of washing the second car is only $2.

Note that the marginal cost of washing the third car is $2.50. The marginal cost is higher than that of the second car, yet it is still lower than the marginal cost of the first car. With the third car, we are beginning to see the *law of diminishing marginal returns*. We already established that the teenagers could opt to have one person wash each car, but it was more efficient to divvy up the responsibilities. With three cars per hour, it is still more efficient to spread out the responsibilities than to have each teenager wash one car individually, but the advantage is getting smaller.

Now examine the marginal cost of the fourth car. Because the three teens are trying to wash four cars at the same time, the marginal cost is not only rising, but is higher than that of the first car. The trend of rising marginal cost continues with each successive car. This illustrates economic theory regarding marginal cost. Initially, the marginal cost falls as production increases. But eventually, the law of diminishing marginal returns sets in. From that point forward, the marginal cost of each unit rises.

The average total cost is the sum of the fixed and variable costs divided by the number of cars washed. If we examine the average total cost column, we will see other cost patterns emerge. Notice how the average cost falls throughout the first five cars and then begins to rise with the sixth car. To understand why, compare the average total cost and marginal cost. The total cost of washing one car is $13, implying an average cost of $13 per car. Because the marginal cost associated with a second car is only $2, we can assume the average cost of washing two cars will be less than the average cost of washing one car. We can infer that the average cost will continue to fall as long as the marginal cost of the next car is below the average. Indeed, because the marginal cost of the third car is $2.50, the average cost of three cars falls from $7.50 to $5.83.

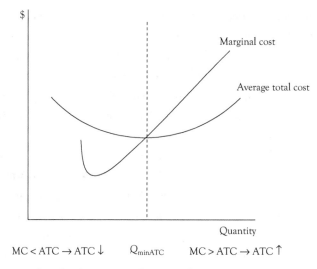

Figure 2.4 Graph of a marginal cost and an average total cost curve

This is why the average total cost does not rise until the sixth car. Even though marginal cost is rising, it is still below the average, pulling the average down. But because the average cost of washing five cars is $5.20 and the marginal cost of the sixth car is $7, the sixth car will cause the average cost to rise.

A generic graph of a firm's marginal and average total cost curves is illustrated in Figure 2.4. The upward-sloping portion of the marginal cost curve corresponds to the law of diminishing marginal returns in production. The average total cost curve is U-shaped. The average total cost falls until production reaches Q_{minATC}. This is because the marginal cost is less than the average of the total cost. Beyond Q_{minATC}, the marginal cost exceeds the average total cost, causing the average total cost to rise.

Production and Pricing Decisions

Let's put the pieces together to see how the profit-maximizing price and output are determined. When deciding whether to produce a given unit of output, the firm needs to determine the marginal revenue and the marginal cost. The marginal revenue is the change in revenue that is associated with the increase in production, whereas the marginal cost is the increased cost associated with the increase in production. Logically, if the increase in revenue is greater than the increase in cost, the unit will add to the firm's profits. Thus, the firm will maximize profits by producing every unit for which the marginal revenue exceeds the marginal cost, and will produce no unit for which its marginal cost is greater than its marginal revenue.

If we incorporate economic theory, we can see these forces take shape. The law of demand states that the more output the firm wants to sell, the lower the price it must charge. The marginal revenue of an additional unit of output is the sum of the output and price effects. The output effect is the revenue generated by the additional output. The price effect is the decrease in revenue that occurs because the price was lowered for the other units. The marginal cost is the additional cost associated with producing the additional output. Theory suggests that the marginal cost should fall initially, but that it should begin to rise once the law of diminishing marginal returns in production sets in.

Let's return to the case of the teenagers hoping to raise money by washing cars. Table 2.5 creates a demand schedule and combines it with the cost information in Table 2.4. Recall that the context was determining how many cars to wash each hour. The teenagers know that the lower the price they charge, the more the number of cars they can manage in the hour. They also know that washing more cars incurs higher variable costs.

We can determine the profit-maximizing price and output if we simply focus on the marginal revenue and marginal cost columns. We will begin by assuming that if the teens charge more than $10, they will not

Table 2.5 Determining the profit-maximizing price and output

Cars	Price	Total revenue	Marginal revenue	Total cost	Marginal cost	Average total cost
0	$11	$0	—	$10	—	
1	$10	$10	$10	$13	$3	$13
2	$9	$18	$8	$15	$2	$7.50
3	$8	$24	$6	$17.50	$2.50	$5.83
4	$7	$28	$4	$21	$3.50	$5.25
5	$6	$30	$2	$26	$5	$5.20
6	$5	$30	$0	$33	$7	$5.50

be able to attract any cars. If they set a price of $10, they will attract one car per hour. Although the total cost of washing one car is $13, $10 of that is a fixed cost that will be spent anyway. The added cost is only $3. Therefore, because the teenagers have already purchased the washing liquid and sponges (and presumably cannot return them), the teens are better off charging $10 and losing $7 in the fundraiser than not attracting any business at all.

Because the fundraiser is doomed to lose money if they charge $10, they must consider whether to lower the price to $9, which they believe is necessary to attract two cars per hour. Two cars will generate revenues of $18. However, the marginal revenue is only $8 due to the price effect. In other words, although the teens will get nine additional dollars from washing the second car, they lose a dollar from the car that could have been washed at a price of $10. The marginal cost of the second car is $2. If the teens drop their price to $9, their revenues will increase by $8 while their costs rise by $2. This implies that the fundraiser will generate an additional $6 by lowering their price by enough to attract a second car.

By examining the total revenue and total cost information on Table 2.5, we can see that the car wash generates a profit at this price. Revenues total $18, whereas costs sum to $15. If the teens charge $9 for a car wash, the fundraiser will earn a $3 profit.

Of course, the objective of the teens is to maximize profits, not simply to generate one. Thus, whereas they can charge $9, attract two cars, and earn a $3 profit, they may decide to lower the price to $8 and attract three cars. As Table 2.5 indicates, by lowering the price to $8, revenues will increase by $6. Because the marginal cost of the third car is only $2.50, the table indicates that they will increase profits by $3.50 if they lower the price to $8.

We can see this more directly by comparing the total revenue and total cost on the table. We already noted that their total profit would be equal to $3 if they set a price of $9 and attracted two cars. By lowering the price to $8 and attracting three cars, the total profit is $24 minus $17.50 or $6.50. As implied by the simple comparison of the marginal revenue and marginal cost, by attracting three cars, the total profits rise from $3 to $6.50, or an increase of $3.50.

The pricing and production decisions continue in this fashion. The teenagers must determine how many cars they want to wash to maximize profits. The more cars they want to attract, the lower the price they must charge. Similarly, the more cars they need to wash, the higher the variable costs. As long as the marginal revenue exceeds the marginal cost, the additional car will increase the group's profit. As we can see, for example, the marginal revenue from the fourth car is $4 and its marginal cost is $3.50. This means that the group's profits will rise by $0.50 by washing four cars instead of three.

At this point, the teens are charging $7, attracting four cars, and generating a total profit of $7. According to the table, they could lower the price to $6 and attract five cars. If they do so, their revenue will rise by $2. Their costs, on the other hand, will rise by $5. Clearly, it would make no logical sense to incur additional costs of $5 so they can increase revenues by $2. If they did so, their profit would decline by $3. Indeed, the table shows that would be the case. At a price of $6, the car wash would generate a profit of $4, which is three dollars less than if they charged $7 and only washed four cars.

Figure 2.5 illustrates the profit-maximizing price and output graphically. As the graph indicates, the marginal revenue from each unit of

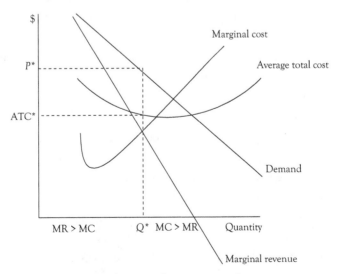

Figure 2.5 The marginal cost and average total cost curve

output exceeds its marginal cost until $Q*$. From that point forward, the marginal cost exceeds the marginal revenue. The profit-maximizing output is, therefore, $Q*$, and the profit-maximizing price is indicated by the corresponding price on the demand curve ($P*$).[3]

The firm's total profit can also be inferred from the diagram. The firm's total revenue is equal to $P*$ times $Q*$. The firm's total cost is equal to $Q*$ multiplied by the average total cost at $Q*$. The firm's total profit, therefore, is equal to ($P* - ATC*$) times $Q*$.

Accounting and Economic Profits

Thus far, our analysis has focused on the firm's choice of a profit-maximizing price and output level in its present industry. In a broader perspective, profit maximization is not limited to the price and output in one's current industry, but rather to the choice of industry.

Economists define opportunity cost as what one has to give up to get something. What is the cost of becoming a professional photographer? One will need a quality digital SLR camera, lenses, camera kit, and cleaning equipment. The aspiring photographer may rent a studio or work out of the home. To market one's work, the photographer may want to put together a portfolio or advertise in the Yellow Pages.

Figure 2.6 shows a representative annual income statement for Heidi. She rents a studio and pays an assistant. She operates her business as a limited liability company.

Assuming the numbers in the income statement are accurate, Figure 2.6 summarizes the costs associated with running her business. But does it?

Heidi does not pay herself a salary. Her personal income is generated by the company's profits. But her business only generated a profit of $18,000. Assuming business is not going to improve appreciably, should Heidi consider getting out of the photography industry?

Unfortunately, this cannot be gleaned from Heidi's income statement. We only know her revenues, an itemized breakdown of her costs, and her profit. Although we assume Heidi could make more money outside of photography, we have no direct evidence to suggest that she should.

Sales:		$120,000
Costs:		
Rent:	$15,000	
Supplies:	$60,000	
Assistant salary:	$25,000	
Advertising:	$2,000	
Total:	$102,000	
Profit before tax:	$18,000	

Figure 2.6 Photographer's annual income statement

But Heidi knows. If she believes she can make a better living elsewhere, it is just a matter of time before she dumps the business. She may tinker with the business; she may investigate better marketing techniques or find ways to operate the business more efficiently, but unless she enjoys photography so much that she's willing to survive on a lower income, we can anticipate that sooner or later, she will leave.

Economists also understand the importance of knowing Heidi's alternatives. For this reason, we consider the opportunity cost of being a photographer is composed of both *explicit costs* and *implicit costs*. Her explicit costs are those detailed in the income statement. They consist of the out-of-pocket expenses necessary to run the business. Heidi's implicit costs include income opportunities that she foregoes by becoming a full-time photographer. Perhaps she quits a job at which she was earning $30,000. Instead of funneling money into her business, she may have invested the funds and earned income from interest and dividends. Maybe she'd be better off in another location. None of these implicit costs show up in Heidi's income statement, but they all play a role in her decision to continue her profession or leave it behind.

To better capture Heidi's thought process, economists adapt the income statement to reveal what is depicted in Figure 2.7. They refer to Heidi's $18,000 as her *accounting profit*. Although the IRS may not consider Heidi's implicit cost to be relevant, we know that *she* does. Once the foregone salary of $30,000 is included in the income statement and rightfully treated as a cost of being a professional photographer, we can

Sales:		$120,000
Costs:		
Rent:	$15,000	
Supplies:	$60,000	
Assistant salary:	$25,000	
Advertising:	$2,000	
Total:	$102,000	
Accounting profit:	$18,000	
Implicit cost:	$30,000	
Economic loss:	($12,000)	

Figure 2.7 Photographer's income statement

see that although her business is profitable, she is $12,000 worse off than she could be. Economists label the $12,000 as her *economic profit* (which is, in this case, an economic loss).

Of course, if Heidi really enjoys her work, she may be willing to forego some income to do something she really loves. But even that has limits. Indeed, we can assume there is some income figure in Heidi's mind that could lure her permanently out of the photography business. For the sake of simplicity, we will assume that Heidi has no nonpecuniary preferences and will make her decisions strictly based on income.

The economic profit for a firm is simply the difference between its accounting profit and the income it foregoes to operate this business (implicit costs). Hence, if the economic profit is negative (a.k.a. economic loss), as in Heidi's case, we assume the firm will eventually leave the industry. If the economic profit is greater than zero, this industry generates greater profits than any alternative sources of income, causing the firm to choose to remain where it's at. If the economic profit is equal to zero, the accounting profit enjoyed by the firm is exactly equal to its implicit cost. This suggests that whereas the firm has no incentive to leave the industry, it is earning the bare minimum that would allow it to remain there. If the accounting profits were any less, the firm would incur an economic loss and leave the industry. This special situation is called *zero economic profits* or a *normal profit*.

Normal profits are important because they represent the minimum profit necessary to enter an industry. Assuming that Heidi will go wherever the income opportunities are greatest, if she was earning $30,000 per year as a salaried employee, she would require a minimum accounting profit of $30,000 to start her own business. Likewise, she would leave the industry if she inferred that her profits would fall permanently below $30,000.

The concept of economic profits is not really foreign to firms. The cost of capital used in net present value calculations builds implicit costs into capital budgeting decisions. It represents foregone investment income, dividends, or interest expenses that might otherwise remain with the firm. If the net present value is greater than zero, the firm concludes that the project under consideration is more profitable than any alternative use of the funds.

Let's make a minor adaptation to the graph in Figure 2.5. We will assume that the costs depicted in the illustration include not only the explicit costs but also the implicit costs. That would imply that the difference between the firm's total revenue and its total costs represents its economic profit. If so, then the difference between the price (i.e., the revenue per unit) and the average total cost (i.e., the average unit cost) is the economic profit per unit. As seen in Figure 2.8, at Q^*, the price exceeds

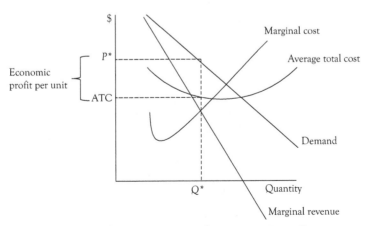

Figure 2.8 Graphical representation of an economic profit

the average total cost. Because the average total cost includes the implicit costs, this firm is earning an economic profit. At a glance, we can see that the firm is earning a profit that exceeds its best alternative.

Introduction to the Five Forces Model

In 1979, Harvard economics professor Michael Porter published "How Competitive Forces Shape Strategy" in the *Harvard Business Review*.[4] In it, he developed the now-famous Five Forces Model that has been used extensively in strategic management to identify attractive markets and manage competition. Some industries, such as security brokers, enjoy significant returns on invested capital, whereas others, such as the airline industry, perpetually struggle.

Porter noted that the returns enjoyed in various industries are not a product of luck or managerial skill, but of five forces that determine an industry's long-term profitability. The greater the collective strength of the five forces, the greater the profitability of the industry and the individual firm.

As illustrated in Figure 2.9, the five forces are as follows:

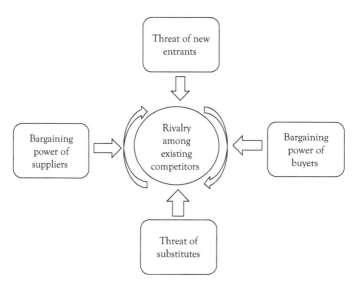

Figure 2.9 The five forces model

1. The threat of substitutes
2. The threat of new entrants
3. The bargaining power of suppliers
4. The bargaining power of buyers
5. The degree of rivalry among existing competitors

This book is dedicated to using economic theory to illustrate the role that each of the five forces plays in a firm's profitability. Each chapter will focus on one of the five forces and use economic theory to demonstrate its impact on a firm's profits.

Summary

- The law of demand forces firms to lower prices to sell additional output. The marginal revenue is the additional revenue generated by the additional output. It is the sum of the output and price effects. The output effect is the revenue generated by the additional unit of output. The price effect is the foregone revenue from lowering the price on the units that would have been produced anyway.
- A firm's costs are composed of fixed costs and variable costs. Fixed costs do not vary with production whereas variable costs vary with production. The marginal cost is the additional cost incurred by an increase in production.
- The marginal cost of production is expected to decrease initially, but eventually it should increase due to the law of diminishing marginal returns.
- A firm will maximize profits by producing every unit for which the marginal revenue exceeds the marginal cost.
- The opportunity cost of operating a business is the sum of its explicit and implicit costs. The explicit costs include the expenses incurred in operating a business. Implicit costs consist of income opportunities that are foregone by operating the business.
- The difference between a firm's revenue and its explicit costs represents its accounting profit. This is the figure represented

in an income statement. The difference between a firm's accounting profit and its implicit costs is called the economic profit. It compares the firm's present accounting profit with foregone income opportunities.

- An economic profit implies that a firm is more profitable in its present industry than in any alternative industry. An economic loss means that the firm would be more profitable in another industry. A normal profit is the minimum accounting profit necessary to remain in a given industry. It implies that a firm's accounting profit is no better or worse than its next best income opportunity.

- The Five Forces Model asserts that the profitability of an industry will depend on the collective strength of five forces: the threat of substitutes, threat of new entrants, bargaining power of suppliers, bargaining power of buyers, and degree of rivalry among existing competitors.

PART II

What Does Five Forces Model Say About Your Firm?

CHAPTER 3

Warning

Cheaper Substitutes Are Hazardous to Your Profits

Availability of Substitutes and Price Elasticity

Price and Performance Trade-off

A firm's biggest challenge is maximizing profits in a world in which consumers have alternatives. Consumers have choices: they can buy an identical product from a rival firm, they can look for reasonable substitutes that offer a better value, or they can do without entirely. Firms need to identify industries in which their income opportunities will be greater and more secure over the long term. They also need proactive strategies that allow them to establish and maintain a competitive advantage for as long as possible.

The first of the Five Forces that we will discuss is the threat of substitute goods. From the consumer's perspective, the price of a good implies opportunity cost. A consumer cannot spend the same money twice. When deciding whether to buy a particular good, the consumer weighs the purchase against alternatives. Not only do consumers compare prices, they also compare product attributes. Some products are more substitutable than others. The closer the substitutes, the greater the role price plays in purchase decisions.

Economists evaluate the role of price and performance trade-offs between available substitutes by adapting the consumer choice model used to derive the law of demand. Recall that the patron was choosing between hot dogs and Coke. Both goods had the same price. In that example, the first item the consumer bought was the hot dog because it gave him more satisfaction than the first Coke. Now let's allow prices to differ. Suppose each hot dog costs \$2 and each Coke costs \$1. Does the consumer continue to buy the hot dog because it gives him more satisfaction, or does he buy the Coke because it's cheaper?

Economists assume consumers undergo a cost and benefit analysis while making purchase decisions. The benefit is the marginal utility associated with obtaining a unit of a given product. The cost is the opportunity cost associated with the purchase, which is represented by the price. Thus, the ratio of the benefits to the costs, or MU/P, shows the marginal satisfaction per dollar spent on that unit.

Let's incorporate this into the hot dog or Coke decision. In deciding whether to buy the first hot dog or the first Coke, the consumer weighs the marginal satisfaction per dollar from buying the first hot dog against the marginal satisfaction per dollar from buying the first Coke. Given that the price of the hot dog is double the price of the Coke, we may infer that the consumer will not buy the hot dog unless it gives him at least twice as much satisfaction as the first Coke. Thus, if the buyer chooses the hot dog, we know that

$$MU_{HD}^{1}/P_{HD} > MU_{C}^{1}/P_{C}$$

At first glance, consumer choice theory may seem to be a little complicated, but the concept is actually quite simple. In choosing between the first hot dog and the first Coke, the ratio of benefits to costs asserts that the consumer will buy the unit that gives him the most for his money. He doesn't necessarily buy the good that provides the most satisfaction nor does he always buy the good that is the cheapest. Instead, he evaluates the price and performance of the available alternatives and chooses accordingly.

We can use the consumer choice model to evaluate the role of substitutes in purchase decisions. Suppose a consumer is choosing between identical cars offered at two dealerships (A and B). Because the cars are identical, the marginal utility of each car will be the same, or $MU_A = MU_B$. If the prices offered at both dealerships are also identical, the consumer will be indifferent to both dealers.[1] In terms of the consumer choice model, consumer indifference between A and B implies

$$MU_A/P_A = MU_B/P_B$$

If the price at dealership A is less than the price at B, the consumer will purchase the car from A because the marginal satisfaction per dollar is greater for A than for B, or

$$MU_A/P_A > MU_B/P_B$$

In other words, if two goods are identical, the consumer will buy the good from the firm that offers the lower price.

Let's go back to assuming the prices are the same. This time, the models are not quite identical. Specifically, the car at dealership A is red (the buyer's preferred color) whereas the car at B is blue. Because the buyer prefers red to blue, the satisfaction derived from the A dealership is greater than that obtained from the B car, or $MU_A > MU_B$. If the prices are the same, the consumer will purchase the car from A because

$$MU_A/P_A > MU_B/P_B$$

Note the ramifications from the perspective of the dealers. Because the consumer prefers the red car to the blue car, the salesperson at B will have to offer a lower price than the dealer at A. In essence, because $MU_A > MU_B$, the salesperson at dealership B needs to lower the price until

$$MU_B/P_B > MU_A/P_A$$

If the prospective buyer has a mild preference for red, the discounted price offered by B will not have to be as great as if the individual had a strong preference for red (or a strong disdain for blue).

We can expand on this model to include a variety of options. In addition to his color preference, suppose the buyer has a strong preference for a car with automatic transmission. The car at dealership B has a standard transmission. This increases the discount necessary to get the consumer to buy from B rather than A.

Let's reverse the perspective to reflect that of the salesperson at dealership A. When the models were identical, the buyer was going to purchase the car from the dealership that offered the best price. But because A offers the buyer's preferred color and transmission, it does not have to match B's offer to make the sale. It merely has to offer a price that makes its model a better overall buy relative to B's model. In terms of the Five Forces, consumer choice theory offers the following insight: the closer the substitutes, the greater the role that price competition plays in consumer decisions.

Price Elasticity of Demand

To help us understand how the threat of substitute impacts the firm, we will develop the concept of the *price elasticity of demand*. The law of demand asserts that as the price of a good rises, the quantity demanded decreases and vice versa. The price elasticity of demand takes the basic law one more step: It refers to the degree to which the quantity demanded responds to price changes.

Let's illustrate the concept of price elasticity graphically. Figure 3.1 shows the demand curves for gasoline and frozen yogurt. Note that whereas the law of demand holds in both cases, a given increase in the price leads to a larger decrease in the quantity of frozen yogurt demanded relative to the decline in the quantity of gasoline demanded. When the quantity demanded of a given product is relatively responsive to price changes (i.e., frozen yogurt), we say that good has a relatively *elastic* demand. When the quantity demanded of a good is not very responsive to price changes (i.e., gasoline), we say the good has a relatively *inelastic* demand.

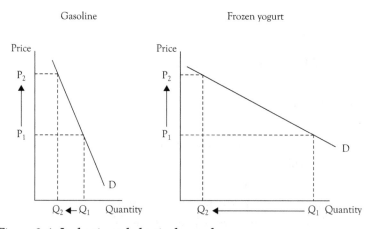

Figure 3.1 Inelastic and elastic demand curves

Because the law of demand holds in either case, how does one distinguish elastic from inelastic? Economists define a good as having an elastic demand if the percentage change in the quantity demanded exceeds the percentage change in the price. If the percentage change in the quantity demanded is less than the percentage change in the price, the good has a relatively inelastic demand. If the percentage changes are the same (i.e., a 10 percent price increase leads to a 10 percent decrease in the quantity demanded), the good is said to have a *unitary* demand.

The availability of substitutes is a primary determinant of price elasticity. Consumers look to minimize the opportunity cost of making a purchase. When the price of a good rises, they look for cheaper substitutes. Thus, when the price of frozen yogurt rises, they can substitute frozen yogurt with ice cream. In contrast, a car runs only on gasoline. If the price of gas rises, drivers cannot pump a cheaper substitute into their tanks.

The rising availability of substitutes spelled doom for the Borders Group. Created in 1971 by Tom and Louis Borders, the company became the nation's second-largest megabook chain behind Barnes & Noble, boasting 1,200 retail outlets worldwide by 2005. But times rapidly began to change in the book industry. In addition to the growing popularity of online shopping spearheaded by Amazon, e-books rapidly became a cheap substitute for traditional hard copies. Amazon, whose online shopping already made a sizable dent in the book market, introduced the Kindle in 2007 to capitalize on the newer, cheaper substitute. Two years later, Barnes & Noble entered the e-book market when it launched its Nook.[2] By the end of 2010, Amazon's e-book downloads outnumbered its sales of hard copies.[3] Barnes & Noble quickly captured 27 percent of the e-book market, selling three times as many e-books as online hard copy book sales.[4]

But Borders lagged behind the others. It partnered with Kobo, Inc. to begin offering e-readers in 2010.[5] By then, it was too late. In February 2011, the firm filed for Chapter 11 bankruptcy and began closing its outlets. The last door was closed seven months later.

The growing availability of substitutes also forced Blockbuster into bankruptcy in 2010. Launched in 1985, the company sought to profit from the growing video rental market that accompanied the rising popularity of VCRs. When DVD players replaced VCRs as the viewing medium of choice, DVDs replaced videocassettes. But as the market environment changed, Blockbuster began to unravel. Netflix emerged with its DVD-by-mail service, which eliminated the consumer hassle of having to return the DVD to the retail outlet after viewing. Redbox offered kiosks at supermarkets and convenience stores, offering consumers a chance to rent current DVDs cheaply as they made other purchases. Online downloading became another viable substitute for the conventional outlet rental. Competing rental retail outlets had already closed up shop, leaving Blockbuster as the only national video retail chain by 2010. But the advent of cheaper and more convenient substitutes made retail rentals a dying industry. Like Borders, Blockbuster was too slow to adapt to the emerging substitutes and filed for Chapter 11 bankruptcy in September, 2010.

Firms should not delude themselves into thinking that they have a permanent upper hand over consumers because of a lack of available substitutes. Because the price of a good represents opportunity cost, buyers constantly seek ways to minimize the opportunity cost of a purchase. Firms that foolishly believe they have the advantage over consumers will eventually find that buyers found a way to lower their opportunity costs. When the price of gas increased by $0.86 per gallon between the spring of 2010 and 2011, both Toyota and Honda reported significant increases in Prius and Insight sales.[6] Clearly, most consumers are not in a position to buy a new car when gas prices rise. However, if fuel prices remain high, over time, consumers will look seriously at hybrids when they need a new vehicle. In summary, then, the longer the time the consumer has to make a purchase decision, the more elastic the demand for the good.

Ramifications of Price Elasticity in Price-Setting

Impact on Revenue

In what ways does the threat of substitutes affect price-setting? We will begin by asserting that the closer the substitute, the more elastic the demand. How does pricing a good with a relatively elastic demand differ from that of one with a relatively inelastic demand?

Let's examine the impact of price elasticity on revenue. Assume a firm is currently charging $5 and sells 100 units per day. The law of demand asserts that if it raises its price to $10, the number of units it will be able

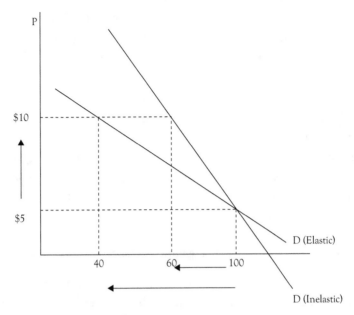

Figure 3.2 Elasticity and revenue

to sell will fall. If the quantity falls to 60 units, the firm's revenue will rise from $500 to $600. If the quantity demanded falls to 40 units, on the other hand, the firm's revenue will fall from $500 to $400.

The various combinations of prices, quantities demanded, and revenue are depicted in Figure 3.2. As the figure illustrates, the scenario in which a higher price leads to an increase in revenue corresponds to the more inelastic demand curve. When the demand curve is relatively elastic, the same price increase leads to the less revenue.

If we reflect on the definitions of elasticity and inelasticity, the relationship between prices and revenue becomes more apparent. Recall that demand is deemed to be elastic if the percentage change in the quantity demanded exceeds the percentage change in the price. Under this definition, if the price rises by 10 percent, the quantity demanded will fall by more than 10 percent. If so, an increase in the price will lead to decrease in revenues. The reverse must also be true. Elastic demand implies that a 10 percent price cut will lead the quantity demanded to increase by more than 10 percent. This will cause revenues to rise. In general, therefore, when demand is elastic, price and revenue move in opposite directions.

When demand is relatively inelastic, the percentage change in the quantity demanded is less than the percentage change in the price. Therefore, price increases will be met with greater revenue, whereas price decreases will cause revenues to fall. When demand is inelastic, price and revenue tend to move in the same direction.

Unitary elasticity exists when the percentage change in the quantity demanded is equal to the percentage change in the price. For example, demand is unitary if a 5 percent price decrease leads the quantity demanded to increase by 5 percent. In such cases, the price change and the quantity change cancel out, causing revenues to remain the same.

Ramifications for the Linear Demand Curve

Consider Table 3.1. As the table indicates, each $1 price increase leads to a one-unit decrease in the quantity demanded. Hence, the demand curve is linear. But look at what happens to the revenue as the price increases. Initially, as the price rises, the total revenue rises even as the quantity demanded falls. This would imply that the demand for the good must be inelastic. But after the price exceeds $6, the total revenue begins to decrease. This would imply that the demand is elastic. Moreover, between $5 and $6, revenue is unchanged, suggesting unitary elasticity.

Table 3.1 Elasticity and the linear demand curve

Price	Quantity demanded	Total revenue	
$1	10	$10	
$2	9	$18	Total revenue rises as the price rises
$3	8	$24	
$4	7	$28	
$5	6	$30	Total revenue is unchanged as the price rises
$6	5	$30	
$7	4	$28	Total revenue falls as the price rises
$8	3	$24	
$9	2	$18	
$10	1	$10	

For the linear demand curve, demand is relatively inelastic at lower prices, becomes unitary as the price increases, and becomes elastic as the price continues to rise. This is depicted in Figure 3.3. The ramifications for price-setting should be clear. As long as the price is in the inelastic portion of the demand curve, an increase in the price will lead to more revenue. Once the price reaches the elastic segment, any subsequent price increase will cause revenues to fall. Hence, the firm will maximize revenues by setting its price in the unitary segment of the demand curve. At this price ($P*$ in the figure), $Q*$ will be demanded.

But doesn't Figure 3.3 run contrary to our discussion on the impact of substitutes on price elasticity? Hardly. Consider Table 3.2. Here, due to the availability of close substitutes, each $1 price increase leads to a two-unit decrease in the quantity demanded, as opposed to the one-unit

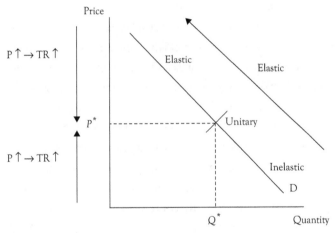

Figure 3.3 Elasticity and the revenue-maximizing price

Table 3.2 Elasticity and the linear demand curve

Price	Quantity demanded	Total revenue	
$1	10	$10	
$2	8	$16	Total revenue rises as the price rises
$3	6	$18	
$4	4	$16	Total revenue falls as the price rises
$5	2	$10	

decrease in Table 3.1. Table 3.2 shows that revenues begin to fall once the price reaches $4. In Table 3.1, where demand was less elastic, revenues did not fall until the price exceeded $6.

The ramifications are important from two perspectives. First, theory suggests that as the price rises, revenues will increase as long as the price is in the inelastic section of the demand curve. Once the price reaches the elastic segment, revenues will fall as the price rises. This implies that firms should not be deluded into thinking that raising the price will cause revenues to rise even if that has been the experience in the past. This would only suggest that the price was still in the inelastic section of demand. Moreover, theory states that the greater the availability of substitutes, the smaller the inelastic section. Thus, the greater the availability of substitutes, the less flexibility the firm has in terms of setting prices.

Apple Corporation's iTunes illustrated the relationship of price elasticity to revenues when it increased the price of many of its songs from $0.99 to $1.29 in 2009. One day after the price increase, 60 songs on its top 100 charts carried a price of $1.29 whereas the remaining 40 were still priced at $0.99. In 24 hours, the $1.29 songs lost an average of 5.3 positions in the charts while the $0.99 songs gained an average of 2.5 positions. The data revealed that the number of downloads for songs whose prices had been raised fell relative to those whose prices remained at $0.99.

But did fewer downloads translate into more or less revenue? According to Nielsen SoundScan data, a #42 song is downloaded roughly 9,800 times over a two-day period.[7] At a price of $0.99, the song generates $9,702 over that time span. In contrast, a #45 song is downloaded approximately 9,200 times over two days. At a retail price of $1.29, the song generates $11,868 over two days. Hence, if raising the price from $0.99 to $1.29 causes the number of downloads to fall from 9,800 to 9,200 over a two-day period, revenues rise by over $2,000. In general, downloads would have to drop by more than 23 percent for the price increase to cause revenues to fall.

Why might demand be inelastic between $0.99 and $1.29? We can examine this from more than one perspective. First, within the iTunes library, songs are certainly not equally desirable. If a consumer is interested in a particular song, another song will not be viewed as an identical substitute or even a reasonably close substitute. The only real issue is whether the consumer likes the song enough to be willing to pay $1.29

to get it. The Billboard data illustrated the law of demand; the number of downloads do fall when prices rise, but largely due to the consumers' willingness to pay, not because the individual is going to substitute into cheaper songs. If Apple continued to experiment with price increases, it would eventually have reached a price that led to a decline in revenues.

The other factor to be considered is the degree to which consumers can obtain the same songs through a source other than iTunes. Compact disks are a substitute for downloads, but the disk requires the consumer to purchase the entire array of songs rather than one at a time. One would be hard-pressed to find a consumer who buys the compact disk to avoid paying the additional $0.30 for the download.

The most significant threat to iTunes to emerge in recent years is music streaming, led by Spotify, Pandora, Last.fm, Deezer, and numerous others. All of the music streaming services offer a free tier of service that is funded by advertisements. The intent, however, is to entice the listener to upgrade to a paid monthly subscription service that is ad-free and offers benefits not available on the free tier. Spotify, for example, allows subscribers to create playlists of songs that they can hear on their computer, tablet, or mobile device. The songs are not downloaded, but as long as the listener can access them at will, the difference between downloading and streaming is unimportant. Spotify offers its premium service for $9.99 per month, making it a preferred alternative to the iTunes user who downloads at least 10 songs (or roughly one album) per month.

The trend toward more streaming and fewer downloads is undeniable. According to the Recording Industry Association of America (RIAA) data, revenue from digital downloads peaked at $2.9 billion in 2012 and dropped to $2.6 billion in 2014. Streaming revenue, on the other hand, increased from $1 billion to $1.9 billion over the same time frame. The trend toward steaming and away from downloading was not missed by Apple, which purchased Beats Music in 2014 as it makes its way into music streaming.[8]

Responses to Changes in Variable Costs

We can also demonstrate how price elasticity impacts the firm's response to changes in variable costs. Logically, a firm would like to respond to an increase in the unit cost by passing it along to the customer. The law of demand, however, suggests that any increase in price will cause fewer units to be demanded. The more elastic the demand, the greater the decrease in the quantity demanded in response to a price hike. This clearly limits the ability of the firm to pass cost increases along to the consumer.

The relationship between unit cost increases, price elasticity, and prices is shown in figures 3.4 and 3.5. Figure 3.4 shows a good with a fairly inelastic demand curve. The vertical distance between the two marginal cost curves is the increase in the unit cost. In response to the increase in the marginal cost, the profit-maximizing price rises, but not by the full

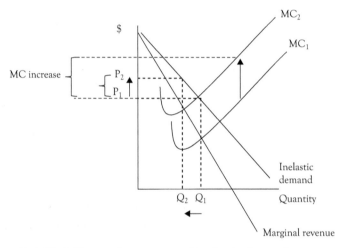

Figure 3.4 Variable cost increases and inelastic demand

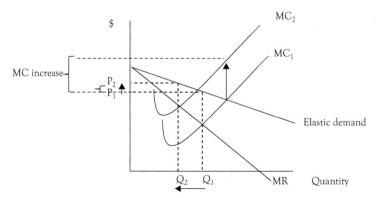

Figure 3.5 Variable cost increases and inelastic demand

amount of the unit cost increase. One can also see that in response to the higher cost, the profit-maximizing production level falls from Q_1 to Q_2.

Figure 3.5 shows the effect of an identical increase in the marginal cost on a product with a more elastic demand curve. Note that a much smaller percentage of the unit cost increase is passed along to the consumer in the form of higher prices. Also note that the decrease in quantity is larger for the good with the elastic demand relative to the product with the more inelastic demand.

Buyer Switching Costs

The easier it is for consumers to switch brands, the greater the threat posed by the substitute. What search engine do you use when surfing the Internet? Google? Yahoo!? Bing? More importantly, does it matter which one you use? For the most part, you type words into the search engine and are presented with a series of links to web pages. Each search engine has its own design, but by and large, the search engine is the road, not the destination. But from Google's and Yahoo!'s perspective, the road you choose means everything. Consumers use the search engine for free, but advertisers bid on keywords and the ad revenues flow to the firm whose search engine you use. In 2000, Google overtook Yahoo! in market share and never looked back. Today, it holds roughly two-thirds of the search engine market.[9] Yahoo! has dropped to third with less than 15 percent of the market.

Yahoo!'s fall from grace undoubtedly has less to do with product quality and more to do with ease of switching. It costs nothing to switch from one search engine to another. Research suggests that 70 percent of web searchers use more than one search engine.[10] One might assume that brand loyalty among search engines is correlated with user satisfaction, but this hypothesis enjoys limited empirical support.[11] Surveys of search engine switchers reveal that only slightly more than half switched because of dissatisfaction with the initial engine.[12]

Web browsers, which also have low switching costs, exhibit similar patterns. Google Chrome exhibited a constant increase in web browser market share, largely at the expense of Internet Explorer and Firefox.[13] In May 2012, Google Chrome overtook Internet Explorer, and now boasts nearly 34 percent of the market.[14] As with search engines, a web browser is simply the doorway to the Internet. But low switching costs allow a newcomer to gain ground against the incumbents.

Switching costs affect the threat of substitutes. Even if a competitor produces a substitute, the incumbent firm is in a better position to withstand the threat if buyer switching costs are high. But the lower the switching costs, the greater the threat posed by the substitute.

Proactive Strategies for Dealing with the Threat of Substitutes

1. Product differentiation

One must consider substitutes as a continuum that must be evaluated in terms of closeness. Bottled water is a very close substitute for tap water, but Pepsi is a more distant substitute for bottled water. A Kia is a close substitute for a Hyundai, but a Trek bicycle is a distant substitute for a Kia. In general, the closer the substitute, the more elastic the demand curve, and the more sensitive the consumer will be to price changes.

The critical response of firms is to create as much distance as possible between its own products and those of competitors. In essence, the goal is to make the demand for its own good less elastic by making it less substitutable. The most effective means of making one's good less substitutable is through product differentiation.

Consider the evolution of the cell phone.[15] Cell technology had been around since 1973, but the first handheld cellular phone was the Motorola DynaTAC introduced in 1983. Film buffs may recall that this was the model wielded by corporate raider Gordon Gekko in the movie *Wall Street*. The 10-inch long model (not including the antenna) sold for a cool $3,995. What all could it do? Well, it allowed the user to make phone calls from cars and while walking along on the sidewalk.

Motorola followed with smaller versions in the next few years. By the early 1990s, Nokia and BellSouth—IBM entered the market. The IBM Simon was the first smartphone, offering a touchscreen and allowing users to send e-mails and faxes in addition to making phone calls. It sold for $899.

Motorola countered with the first clamshell model, the Motorola StarTAC. The Nokia 8110, often called the banana phone, was featured in the futuristic film *The Matrix*. The Nokia 5110 model soon followed and became a consumer favorite for several years. Later, its 5210 model added durability and a splash-proof casing.

In 1999, Samsung offered the first cell phone with MP3 capability. Nokia followed in the same year with the Nokia 3210, the first cell phone to offer text messaging. One year later, Ericsson introduced the R380, which featured a black-and-white touchscreen partially covered by a flip. Later that year, Ericsson offered the R320, which included a WAP browser.

Nokia countered in 2001 with the 5510, the first cell to include a full QWERTY keyboard and then later introduced the 8310, which offered a fully functioning calendar and FM radio. The same year, Ericsson offered the first cell phone with bluetooth capability. Later that year, Ericsson introduced the T66, which was as long as a cigarette, and the T68, which featured a color screen. Siemens entered the market with its S45, the first cell phone with GPRS to allow Internet access. Nokia's 7650, featured in the movie *Minority Report*, was the first cell phone to include a built-in camera.

In the years that followed, cell phones offered gaming, more megapixels, sleeker designs, and full Internet access. Then, in 2007, Apple introduced the iPhone. The model included an auto-rotate sensor, a touch interface that replaced the QWERTY keyboards, and a number of other features. The iPhone 3G, offered in 2008, allowed users to purchase apps through its Apps Store.

Obviously, the description could go on and on. But let's take a step back and see what happened. Gordon Gekko displayed his "Greed is good" credo by lugging around the $4,000 Motorola DynaTAC (which could just as easily be referred to nowadays as the DynaSaur). It was large and had virtually no features. In sharp contrast, Apple's iPhone 4S runs rings around the DynaTAC in terms of features, yet it sells for one-tenth of the price. Shouldn't a superior model be more expensive?

Two key points are important to note: first, each innovation was an attempt to make the competitors' models less substitutable, thereby giving the innovator a less elastic demand curve and more price flexibility. Yet each innovation invited competitors to replicate it, eliminating some of the distance between competing models, making demand more elastic, and reducing some to the price flexibility that had inspired the innovation in the first place. Of course, technological improvements accompanied the introduction of features, allowing manufacturers to compete in terms of both price and features. Hence, cell phones got better, added more features, and ironically, got cheaper. Aside from its nostalgic value, Motorola could not give away its DynaTAC model today.

This brings to light the second key point. Product differentiation is a dynamic process. Each innovation creates temporary distance between the firm's good and that offered by its competitors. Good ideas will be replicated and price flexibility will be lost. Efforts to create a more inelastic demand curve are often short lived. Each innovation must often be followed by a new one. This can be accomplished by adding features and attributes or even as simple as creating brand recognition through advertising. Why does Tylenol products advertise when generics are biochemically identical?

Firms must also be cognizant that viable substitutes can arise quickly. As cell phones became popular, the demand for traditional long-distance phone service practically disappeared. E-mailing capabilities made sending letters obsolete. Social networking and text messaging are quickly turning web-based e-mails into nostalgia. Movie and music downloading carved a large hole in the compact disk and DVD purchase and rental markets. Borders went out of business because it was too slow to adapt to downloading books.

Online shopping has also changed the perception of who one's competitors really are. In the pre-Internet days, consumers shopped at traditional brick-and-mortar stores. This allowed firms to identify competitors as stores with a similar mission. Walmart competed in the mass merchandise market with Kmart while Best Buy competed in the consumer electronics market with Circuit City. But online consumers tend to shop for products rather than browse through stores. In the online marketplace, Best Buy competes with Walmart in the market for televisions and laptop computers. As information technology changes, firms must develop a keener eye for the threat of substitutes, not only in terms of the products themselves, but in the firms whose products may be increasingly viewed as competitors.[16]

Online shopping also forces brick-and-mortar stores to deal with showrooming.[17] The consumers visit the local retailer to compare brands in person, but then retreat to their computers to find the best online price. In essence, consumers free-ride on the display costs borne by the brick-and-mortar retailer and then use the information to buy the good from an online retailer at a lower price. Some retailers, such as Target, try to respond to showrooming by asking vendors to match any online price uncovered by online shoppers. Alternatively, they ask suppliers to create special models that will not be discovered online.

2. Raising buyer switching costs

An important component of the threat of substitutes is consumer switching costs. The easier it is to switch to a competing brand, the more elastic the substitute. It's virtually costless to switch brands of toilet paper. At the other extreme, once an office staff has been trained to use Microsoft Office, it is costly to purchase a competing package and go through the expense of retraining them.

Hence, one proactive strategy may be to raise customer switching costs. In theory, the switching costs associated with mobile service should be fairly low. After all, a Verizon phone call is going to sound just like an AT&T call. But mobile service partners with cell phone manufacturers to offer substantial discounts on cell phones in exchange for a long-term contract. Apple's iPhone 6 with 16 GB retails through the Apple website for $649. Couple the iPhone with a two-year contract with Verizon, and the phone can be purchased for $199. Once an initial package is purchased, subscribers can get low-cost upgrades by extending their contracts.

Similarly, airlines raised switching costs when they introduced frequent flier programs. As with a mobile service, the flying experience is largely the same regardless of an airline. Consequently, fliers select flights largely on the basis of departure or arrival times and price. By allowing customers to obtain free flights by logging miles, they raise the cost of switching to another airline to save a few dollars.

This can be especially an effective tool to maintain business travelers since the employer rather than the employee usually pays for the airfare.

3. Tying

Tying is another tool for reducing the threat of substitutes. Here, the manufacturer produces a good that requires a manufacturer-specific complementary product. One good is offered at a low price to entice the consumer. The firm's primary profit center comes from the complementary good. Dell Computers offers its basic C1760nw all-in-one printer for roughly $180. But a printer is worthless without cartridges. Dell sells the cartridge tailored to the C1760nw model for $49.99 for black ink and $55.99 for color. Hence, with only four refills, the consumer pays as much for cartridges as he did for the printer. Tying the products together increases the switching costs for the consumer. Although less expensive cartridges may be available, they are not likely to fit the C1760nw. The consumer, therefore, must purchase an entirely different printer in order to switch cartridges.[18]

Summary

- The price elasticity of demand refers to the responsiveness of the quantity demanded to price changes. If the percentage change in the quantity demanded is greater than the percentage change in the price, demand is elastic. If the percentage change in the quantity demanded is less than the percentage change in the price, demand is inelastic. If the percentage change in the quantity demanded is the same as the percentage change in the price, demand is unitary.
- In general, the greater the availability of substitutes, the more elastic the demand. However, even if a lack of substitutes exists in the short term, consumers can be counted on to find ways to reduce the opportunity cost of a purchase. Consequently, the longer the time frame, the more elastic the demand.
- The greater the availability of substitutes, the smaller the percentage of a variable cost increase that can be passed along to the consumer in terms of higher prices.

- If demand is relatively elastic, a higher price will cause revenues to fall. If demand is relatively inelastic, a higher price will result in greater revenues.
- All linear demand curves have an inelastic section (at lower prices), a unitary section, and an elastic section (at higher prices). Firms will maximize revenues by setting the price in the unitary section. The greater the availability of substitutes, the smaller the inelastic section of the demand curve. Consequently, the greater the availability of substitutes, the less flexibility the firm has in terms of increasing the price to raise revenues.
- Firms can reduce the threat of substitutes through product differentiation. However, they must keep in mind that successful innovations will be replicated, reducing the firm's price flexibility.
- Low switching costs can also increase the threat of substitutes. Firms may consider strategies to raise switching costs as a means of retaining price flexibility.

CHAPTER 4

We Could Make More Money If Our Competitors Would Just Go Away

Eroding Profits in the Long Run

A second constraint on a firm's long-term profitability is the threat of new entrants. Earlier, we discussed the economics underlying the firm's profit-maximizing price and quantity. We also distinguished between accounting profits (the difference between revenues and costs) and economic profits (the difference between accounting profits and foregone profit opportunities). In this chapter, we will revisit these concepts and show the impact of market entry.

A firm has an economic profit if its accounting profit exceeds any of its income-generating alternatives. Let's create an example. Teddy attended culinary school in Missouri. While studying, he became interested in Thai cuisine and spent six months in Bangkok studying under a master chef. He returned to his hometown and opened its first Thai restaurant. Residents dining out can choose from Italian to Mexican to American cuisine, but Teddy has the town's only Thai restaurant. His restaurant rapidly gains popularity and soon becomes one of the busiest restaurants in town. Although an entrée only incurs average meal and labor costs of $2.50, Teddy is able to charge $15 for meals due to the popularity of the restaurant.

Details of Teddy's income statement for the most recent year appear in Table 4.1. As the table indicates, Teddy earns an annual profit of $512,690. Previously, his household income totaled $125,000. Hence, his economic profit is equal to $387,690.

Table 4.1 Annual income statement for thai restaurant

Total revenue:		$810,000
Total variable costs:		
Meals:	$44,550	
Labor:	$90,450	$135,000
Profit contribution:		$675,000
Occupancy costs:		
Rent:	$96,000	
Equipment rental:	$11,110	
Real estate tax:	$24,000	
Personal property tax:	$6,000	
Insurance:	$18,000	
Liquor liability:	$7,200	$162,310
Accounting profit:		$512,690
Implicit cost:		$125,000
Economic profit:		$387,690

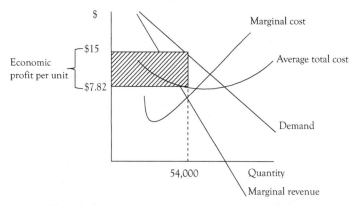

Figure 4.1 Economic profit of Thai restaurant

A generic graph of Teddy's restaurant appears in Figure 4.1. Teddy's profit-maximizing price and number of annual meals are depicted as $15 and 54,000, respectively. The average total cost ($7.82) is the sum of his variable costs, his occupancy costs, and his implicit cost divided by the number of meals: ([$135,000+$162,310+$125,000]/54,000 = $7.82). Hence, the difference between the price and average cost of a meal represents the amount of his economic profit per meal. The shaded area represents his overall economic profit, which in this case is $387,690.

Economic theory predicts that Teddy's success is going to have a relatively short life. In time, others will want to open Thai restaurants in town. How will this affect Teddy's business? Keep in mind that as long as Teddy owns the town's only Thai restaurant, the competing restaurants are rather distant substitutes. But if two or three other Thai restaurants are available, Teddy will have to share this niche of the dining-out market.

How will the competition affect Teddy's business? Diners who prefer Thai food may either choose Teddy's restaurant or one of the other Thai restaurants in the town. Therefore, the demand for meals at Teddy's restaurant will decrease. In addition, because the competitors' food is a closer substitute than what had previously been available in town, the demand for meals at Teddy's restaurant will also become more elastic. Figure 4.2 shows the impact of competing Thai restaurants on Teddy's business.

Figure 4.2 is a little messy, so we'll focus on individual elements one by one. When Teddy has this niche of the market to himself, the demand for meals at his restaurant was represented by the dotted demand curve D_1 and its accompanying dotted marginal revenue curve MR_1. At the profit-maximizing price and quantity ($15 and 54,000, respectively), the price exceeded the average total cost, indicating an economic profit.

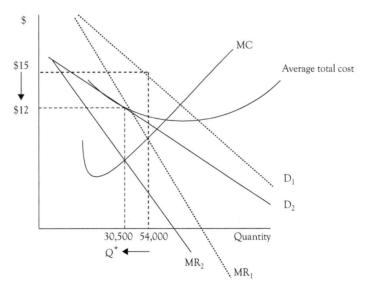

Figure 4.2 Effect of market entry on Teddy's restaurant

The economic profit creates an incentive for competitors to open a Thai restaurant. Because diners may either go to Teddy's restaurant or one of the other Thai restaurants in town, the demand for meals at Teddy's restaurant decreases, and the demand becomes more elastic (the solid lines D_2 and MR_2, respectively). The decline in demand drives the price of Teddy's meals to $12 with an accompanying decrease in the number of meals served (from 54,000 to 30,500).

Table 4.2 shows the impact of market entry on Teddy's income statement. As the table indicates, revenues and variable costs decline due to the lower price and number of meals. Occupancy costs are unchanged. The accounting profits at the restaurant decrease from their previous level of $512,690 to $125,000. In the long run, Teddy's profit from the Thai restaurant is exactly equal to his household income prior to owning the restaurant. In other words, market entry eliminates Teddy's economic profit, leaving him with a normal profit.

Of course, the numbers in tables 4.1 and 4.2 were rigged to tell a story, but the tale is an important one. Economic profits create an incentive to enter the industry. As firms enter the industry, the incumbent firm's demand

Table 4.2 Annual income statement for thai restaurant

Total revenue:		$366,000
Total variable costs:		
Meals:	$25,968	
Labor:	$52,722	$78,690
Profit contribution:		$287,310
Occupancy costs:		
Rent:	$96,000	
Equipment rental:	$11,110	
Real estate tax:	$24,000	
Personal property tax:	$6,000	
Insurance:	$18,000	
Liquor liability:	$7,200	$162,310
Accounting profit:		$125,000
Implicit cost:		$125,000
Economic profit:		$0

decreases and becomes more elastic. This causes the profit-maximizing price and quantity to fall. As long as economic profits continue to exist, firms will enter the industry, driving prices and profits downward. Eventually, when all economic profits are eliminated and incumbent firms are left with a normal profit, market entry will cease. Surviving firms will be left with a normal profit, which, again, is defined as the minimum profit that makes it worthwhile to remain in the industry. Figure 4.3 illustrates the firm in the short run (when it has an economic profit) and in the long run

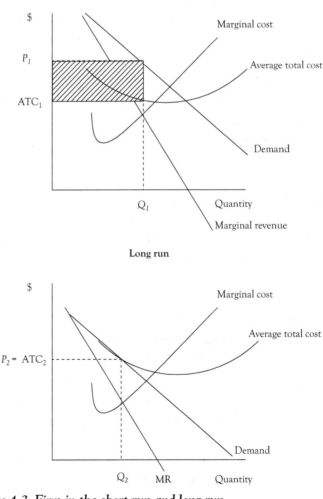

Figure 4.3 Firm in the short run and long run

(when economic profits have been competed away, leaving surviving firms with a normal profit). In the short run, at the profit-maximizing output (Q^*), the price exceeds the average total cost. Because average total cost includes the implicit costs, the firm is enjoying an economic profit. In the long-run graph, after demand has decreased, the price is equal to the average total cost, meaning the firm has a normal profit.

In the case of the Thai restaurant example, how many other Thai restaurants will spring up in town? One more? Two more? One hundred more? This is a critical element in economic theory. An economic profit is a market signal that consumers want more than what is currently available to them. In essence, when Teddy had the only Thai restaurant in town, his economic profit signaled that local residents wanted more. So other culinary entrepreneurs responded to the market signal by creating their own Thai restaurants. Of course, just as Teddy has to share this niche of the market with his competitors, they share the market niche with each other. Assuming that Teddy's operations typify those of the competitors, each time a competitor opens a new Thai restaurant in town, each existing Thai restaurant experiences a decrease in economic profit. Once the economic profits have disappeared entirely, the surviving firms are earning normal profits. At this point, there is no incentive for any other Thai restaurants to open in the town.

We should also note that whereas Teddy's restaurant is less profitable than it once was, he has no incentive to close his restaurant and take up another line of work. A normal profit implies that the accounting profit enjoyed by his restaurant is no more and no less than what he could earn elsewhere. Consequently, even though the restaurant is less lucrative, he has no incentive to leave the industry.

Let's change the scenario a bit. We'll go back to the state of affairs shown in the short-run graph in Figure 4.3. Teddy has the only Thai restaurant in town, and he's earning an economic profit. But this time, prospective competitors are not free to set up shop in Teddy's town. To start their own Thai restaurant, they need a permit from the local government. Conveniently, the individual in charge of reviewing permit applications is Teddy's brother, Freddy. Freddy is a public servant in charge of assuring that restaurant establishments abide by local health codes and that the public interest is served by a new restaurant. And Freddy has high standards for new entrants. So high, in fact, that every single application for a new Thai restaurant has been refused.

How does this change the outlook for Teddy's restaurant? Clearly, the transition from the short-run graph to the long-run graph in Figure 4.3 will not occur. Indeed, the notion that economic profits are inevitably competed away until normal profits exist is predicated on the assumption that market barriers do not exist. If a firm sees an opportunity to make money, one cannot stop it from doing so. But the prospective competitors in Teddy's town do not enjoy the benefits of free market entry. Freddy's restrictive licensing policy constitutes a market barrier. As long as market barriers keep competitors out of Teddy's market, he will continue to charge P_1, sell Q_1 meals, and earn an economic profit.

Sources of Market Barriers

Control Over a Key Resource

Economic theory states that unless market barriers are present, an economic profit cannot last. Market entrants will compete economic profits away, leaving the survivors with a normal profit. Most market barriers are not within the firm's control. However, if a single firm owns most of the resources needed to produce the good, competitors would have difficulty entering the industry.

A modern-day example of a firm that wields a great deal of market power for this reason is De Beers, the South African diamond company. Created in 1871 by Cecil Rhodes, De Beers owned all of the country's diamond mines by 1888. When Rhodes died in 1902, De Beers controlled 90 percent of the world's diamond production. Ernst Oppenheimer took control of the company in 1927. Throughout the twentieth century, the firm took advantage of its market power. It persuaded independent operators to join its cartel, and it flooded the market with diamonds similar to those produced by competitors who did not want to join. When diamond prices were falling, it would stockpile diamonds in order to restrict the market supply and boost prices.

As the twentieth century came to an end, De Beers gradually lost its stronghold on the world supply. Producers in Russia, Canada, and

Australia began distributing diamonds outside De Beers' system. As a result, De Beers market share dropped from 85 to 65 percent. The firm responded by ceding control of the market and concentrating on marketing and branding. In 2011, the Oppenheimer family sold 40 percent of its ownership to Anglo American PLC, thereby ending its century-long hold on the diamond market.

Economies of Scale

Economies of scale exist when production increases lead to long-run declines in the average total cost. Economic theory suggests that in most industries, production increases lead to economies of scale only up to a point. Eventually, *diseconomies of scale* set in, causing the average total cost to rise as production increases.

In some industries, however, economies of scale can exist for significant levels of production. This generally occurs when variable costs are negligible. An example appears in Table 4.3. Fixed costs are assumed to be $10,000 and variable costs are $1 per unit. Thus, as production increases, the average total cost continues to fall.

The advantages of economies of scale should be obvious. According to Table 4.3, a single firm could service 1,000 customers and charge a price as low as $11. In contrast, if 10 competing firms each serviced 100 customers, each one would need to charge at least $101 to survive.

The initial entrant into the market has a significant advantage due to its economies of scale in production. A potential competitor has to make a substantial capital outlay to enter the industry, but realizes that the incumbent firm can take advantage of its economies of scale to charge

Table 4.3 Example of economies of scale

Quantity	Total fixed cost	Total variable cost	Total cost	Average total cost
1	$10,000	$1	$10,001	$10,001
2	$10,000	$2	$10,002	$5,001
10	$10,000	$10	$10,010	$1,001
100	$10,000	$100	$10,100	$101
1,000	$10,000	$1,000	$11,000	$11

a price the new entrant may have difficulty matching. Because the market barriers are weighty, industries with these characteristics are often monopolies. As their monopoly status arises from the unique characteristics of the industry, they are usually referred to as *natural monopolies*.

Table 4.3 should make it obvious that a natural monopoly may be beneficial to the consumer. This firm could service 1,000 customers at a price that is substantially lower than could be charged by two or more competing firms. However, granting a monopoly to a firm may be problematic. Rather than pass along its cost advantages to customers in terms of lower prices, the firm could take advantage of its lack of competition and charge higher prices than might be present under competition. For this reason, natural monopolies are sometimes subject to regulation.

The quintessential example of a natural monopoly is the utilities industry. The infrastructure required to service a town with electricity is considerable. Yet the marginal cost of adding a single customer is quite small. Consequently, most towns are serviced by single utilities company whose rates are regulated by the government.

Substantial economies of scale need not go the extreme of the utilities industry to be a market barrier. The greater the economies of scale in production or the larger the initial capital investment on the front end, the greater the market barriers. Not all firms have easy access to start-up expenditures, either in terms of equity or access to credit. New entrants must also be able to finance start-up losses that are likely to be initially incurred. Large capital investments and start-up losses inject additional risk and may serve as a deterrent to market entry.

Economies of scale may stem from demand as well as supply. *Network effects* refer to goods whose value depends on the number of persons using them. Consumers wishing to participate in online auctions are likely to go to eBay because the number of potential buyers is large. The value of online social networks such as Facebook and Twitter increases as more persons set up accounts.

Sometimes incumbent firms enjoy advantages that are independent of scale. They may have geographical advantages, well-established brand identities, or a built-in trust factor that may make it difficult for prospective competitors to successfully penetrate the market.

Limited Access to Distribution Channels

To get from the manufacturer to the consumer, goods must have access to wholesalers and retailers. Newcomers must displace established brands on the retailers' shelves. Limited access to distribution channels can serve as a market barrier. For years, it was common practice for music companies to pay performers to play their songs. By the 1950s, the practice was extended to radio stations, as music companies paid disk jockeys to give their songs airplay. Subsequent Congressional hearings revealed that the practice of payola was widespread.[1] In 1960, amendments to the Communications Act pronounced payola a crime. The scandals arose because record sales were indelibly tied to airplay and distribution channels and payola limited access.

Music streaming is changing the landscape of artist exposure. Artists can sidestep radio airplay by paying music distribution companies such as TuneCore to deliver their songs to music streamers such as Spotify or Pandora.

Patents and Copyrights

Patents and copyrights represent two kinds of government-created market barriers. Theory allows for inventions and creative works to be protected for similar reasons. Suppose, for example, that copyright laws did not exist. In 1995, J.K. Rowling completed her manuscript for *Harry Potter and the Philosopher's Stone*. In the absence of copyright laws, publishers could simply reproduce the book verbatim and sell it on their own, with no legal obligation to pay Rowling for the rights. Only a small percentage of the proceeds would wind up in Rowling's hands. Given the time and attention needed to write a book, one would have to question whether the subsequent six Harry Potter books would have ever been written.

Copyright protection is not limited to traditional literary works. As computer software became increasingly copied, Congress added the definition of computer program to Title 17 (which defines copyright laws) in 1980. Coupled with court decisions such as *Apple v. Franklin*, computer programs were treated as literary works under the Copyright Act.

Much of Microsoft's market power may be attributed to the fact that its Windows Operating System is copyrighted.

Technological changes over the past 20 years have jeopardized the survival of newspapers. During World War I, the International News Service (INS) gathered Associated Press (AP) stories, rewrote them, and telegraphed the rewritten stories to California newspapers. As the stories reached the West Coast at roughly the same time as the original version, the AP found that it was competing against itself. Although the Supreme Court ruled that INS could not compete against AP by taking its stories and rewriting them, the 1976 Copyright Act made sweeping changes that largely negated the ruling in the INS—AP case.[2]

These changes had no meaningful effect on the newspaper industry until the last decade. In the days when newspapers required the use of printing presses, the notion that someone would buy up newspapers, rewrite the stories, and circulate them through their own newspapers didn't pose much of a threat. By the time the rewritten stories became available, the commercial value of the news was largely gone.

Technology has changed that. Today, news aggregators and bloggers can obtain new stories from major media using RSS feeds, rewrite the stories, use automated mechanisms such as Google AdSense to sell ads around the stories, and get them online by the time readers log onto their computers in the morning. Given the automated nature of the RSS feeds and programs such as AdSense, market barriers are extremely low.

The result was similar to AP's experiences with INS during World War I. Newspapers were expending a large sum of money on reporters to acquire stories only to find themselves competing against their own rewritten stories prepared by free-riding aggregators.

In the face of such competition, a number of longstanding newspapers such as the *Cincinnati Post*, the *Tucson Citizen*, and the *Albuquerque Tribune* have ceased to operate over the last five years. Others, such as the *Detroit Free Press* and the New Orleans *The Times-Picayune* have slashed their staffs and reduced the frequency of their publications.[3]

Patent protection exists for reasons similar to the rationale for copyright laws. The patent allows the inventor to be the sole manufacturer and seller of the good for a period of 20 years. Pharmaceutical companies often obtain patents from the government on new discoveries. The typical pharmaceutical company expends a great deal of money on research and development in the hope it can invent a new drug. If patents did not exist, competing companies could purchase the drug, have chemists determine the chemical ingredients, and market the same drug as a competing brand. Prices would reflect the ongoing operating costs involved in manufacturing and selling the drug, but it's questionable as to whether the firm that invented the drug would be able to recover its R&D expenses. This suggests that it would be a wiser strategy to wait for someone else to invent the good than to invent it yourself. The patent allows the inventor to recoup its investment by permitting it to charge a higher price than would have been charged in the presence of competition. But the patent protection is temporary: after 20 years, any firm can produce and sell the good.

In late 2012, two of the patents owned by Green Mountain Coffee Roasters expired. Green Mountain created the Keurig coffeemakers that dispense single servings of coffee through K-cups. Knowing that its innovation is relatively easy to replicate, the company saw the writing on the wall and began protecting itself against the onslaught of competition. Assuming coffee-drinkers are likely to be brand-loyal, the firm established partnership agreements to cobrand with various coffeemakers, including Caribou Coffee, Dunkin' Donuts, and Folgers, to steer consumers back into K-cups.

But that was not enough. In addition to competition from single-serving coffee dispensers, firms created reusable K-cups that were a significant threat to Green Mountain's one-and-done K-cup. Some simple math will show the difference. A package of 16 to 18 K-cups, containing 0.35 ounces of coffee, typically sells for $11 or $12. Hence, a coffee drinker who has one K-cup per day will spend roughly $12 to get up to 18 days of his coffee fix. A typical bag of coffee, containing roughly 311 grams, sells for $8 or less. As 0.35 ounces is equal to 10 grams, the bag, which costs one-third less than the package of K-cups, has enough coffee to last a month. More coffee for less money.

Although Green Mountain had its own reusable K-cups, the fact that competitors' products were compatible with their machines implied losing the lucrative K-cup market that amounted to 73 percent of Green

Mountain's net sales.[4] The firm responded by creating a new Keurig 2.0 coffeemaker that has interactive readers that are programmed to work only with Keurig-licensed K-cups.

Licensing

Another government-established market barrier is licensing. In many industries, an entrepreneur with the know-how and drive to produce a good or service can simply do so. In other industries, the individual must obtain a license from the government to operate the business.

The economic rationale for licensing deals with informational asymmetries.[5] Markets work best when consumers are well informed. In most cases, buyers are in a sound position to evaluate a purchase. If they are dissatisfied, they won't return to the same merchant. If the number of dissatisfied customers is sufficiently large, the merchant will go out of business.

In some industries, however, it isn't particularly easy for the consumer to discern a high-quality establishment from a low-quality one. If an individual loses in a civil court case, does that imply that his attorney is incompetent? Given that there is one winner and one loser in every case that goes to trial, even if the attorneys arguing the case are highly skilled, one of them will lose. Similarly, if the economy unexpectedly turns sour, even the most savvy stockbroker cannot protect his client from an investment portfolio gone bad. In such cases, licensing can serve a valuable function by signaling a minimum level of competency to prospective customers.

At the same time, occupational licensing is one of the most frequently criticized practices by economists. In the name of consumer protection, it creates barriers to potential competitors. Market barriers drive up prices and increase profits, which can work to the detriment of consumers. From an economic perspective, the yardstick is whether the higher price is justified by the quality signal it sends to consumers. Quite often, those claims are questionable. In Texas, shampoo specialists must take 150 hours of coursework on subjects such as "theory and practice of shampooing."[6] Michigan requires massage therapists to take 500 hours of coursework to become licensed. Ironically, massage therapists who existed before the laws were passed were not required to take such coursework.

One wonders what would be the consequence of an inadequate shampoo job or a massage that did not relieve muscle tension. Do these licensing requirements enhance consumer welfare or protect the earnings of practitioners from competition?

In some cases, the license requires little more than paying a licensing fee. In Massachusetts, for example, a person can become a licensed fortune teller by paying a fee that ranges between $2 and $50 and residing in the town for at least a year prior to applying for the license. Is the purpose of the law to ensure customers that only those who can truly predict the future can practice? Although one can debate the merits of occupational licensing on a case-by-case basis, it serves as a market barrier that raises prices and increases profits.

An interesting battle over the past several years has been waged between mobile-based ridesharing companies, such as Uber, Lyft, and Sidecar, and local taxi and limousine commissions. Unlike the traditional practice of standing at the street corner and hailing a cab, riders can request a ride through an app on their mobile device. The ridesharing company matches the customer with a driver in the area, showing the price. If the rider accepts, the individual sees a picture of the driver, the vehicle's license plate, and can even track the progress of the car as it reaches the patron.

So what's wrong with that? Simple: it's competition for the taxi industry and they haven't taking it lying down. Historically, taxis and limousines existed in a regulated industry, shielding them from competitors such as Uber. Not surprisingly, then, cab companies have cried foul and lobbied, sometimes successfully, to keep ridesharing services out of their cities. Indeed, rarely has Uber entered a market without resistance from taxi companies. Los Angeles, San Francisco, Las Vegas, Miami, New York, and Washington, DC are among the myriad of cities that sponsored legislation or issued cease-and-desist orders to keep ridesharers off the roads. Washington even debated passing the Uber Amendment, which would have required Uber to charge a minimum fare that was at least five times higher than the fare charged by a taxicab. The legal challenges against rideshare companies are not limited to the United States. Germany, Spain, India, Canada, and Brazil are just a few of the many countries to take legal action to keep ridesharers off the taxi and limousine companies' turf.

Government Regulations

Often, government regulations can serve as a deterrent to entry. Some industries are heavily governed by environmental and safety regulations. The 21st Amendment, for example, repealed prohibition, but granted states and local municipalities the right to create their own laws to restrict the sale of alcohol. Until the *Granholm v. Heald* case in 2005, Michigan forbade out-of-state wineries from shipping wine directly to Michigan consumers. Ironically, the law permitted similar shipments from in-state wineries. The U.S. Supreme Court deemed the laws to be unconstitutional. The defense argued that the 21st Amendment allowed for such preferential treatment in alcohol sales.

Trade Restrictions

Trade restrictions bear a great deal of similarity to licensing. They represent laws that curtail competition by foreign firms. Quite often, trade restrictions exist in the name of protecting American jobs, a claim that most economists find spurious. Economists suggest that the real intent of these restrictions is to reduce competition and allow prices and domestic producer profits to rise at the expense of consumers. The International Trade Commission lists over 12,000 U.S. goods that are protected by tariffs, including most vegetables, wool clothing, commercial plateware, and tobacco.[7]

Proactive Strategies for Dealing with the Threat of New Entrants

Limit Pricing

Several of the market barriers discussed so far are largely determined or influenced by factors that lie well beyond the control of an individual firm. Few firms have a significant control over key resources; patents can only be obtained through the United States Patent and Trademark Office and will only be granted if the invention meets the standards that would warrant protection. Industries conducive to a natural monopoly are rare and never unilaterally determined by the firm. Licensing protection and trade restrictions can only occur by successfully lobbying the state and federal government.

One can logically assume that a firm with these characteristics may take advantage of them. But what can a firm do to ward off new entrants if it is not protected by patents, licenses, or government regulation? Frankly, if the financial stakes are large enough, nothing absent direct governmental intervention can stave off competition indefinitely. A more viable strategy, then, is for the firm to erect temporary barriers that might delay the entry of firms.

One means through which a firm can deter entry is through limit pricing. Figure 4.4 shows the firm's short-run profit-maximizing price and output level. As has been discussed, the firm enjoys economic profits represented by the shaded area on the graph. This creates an incentive for competitors to enter the market.

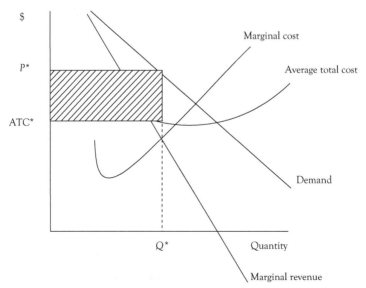

Figure 4.4 Short-run profit-maximizing price and quantity

Suppose, however, that instead of charging the price that maximizes its current profits, the firm charges a lower price. By charging a lower price than what maximizes short-term profits, the firm hopes to deter competitors from entering the market.

To see how this might work, assume the potential entrant has an identical cost structure to the incumbent firm. The incumbent firm lowers its price to P_L, which allows it to sell Q_L units.[8] Because the firm services the entire market at P_L, if a new firm entered the industry and matched the current price, its quantity demanded would be equal to zero. If it entered the industry and undercut the existing firm's price, its quantity demanded would be the excess market demand that is not serviced by the incumbent firm.

Figure 4.5 illustrates the new entrant's demand curve. At the limit price, the incumbent firm produces Q_L and services the entire market. If the new entrant charged P_2, its quantity demanded would be the difference between the market demand and Q_L, which is plotted on the graph as Q_{NP2}. For example, if the incumbent firm produced 1,000 units and the quantity demanded in the market at P_2 was 1,150 units, the quantity demanded for the new entrant at P_2 (noted on the graph as Q_{NP2}) would be 150 units. At a lower price, such as P_3, the excess demand would even be greater. For example, if the market demand at P_3 was equal to 1,250 units, the quantity demanded for the new entrant (Q_{NP3}) would be 250 units. As illustrated in Figure 4.5 at prices P_L, P_2, and P_3, we can sketch a demand curve for the potential entrant.

Figure 4.6 isolates on the new entrant's demand and cost curves. Note that at each price, the potential entrant cannot sell enough units to cover average total cost. This means the firm cannot increase its profits by entering the market, allowing the incumbent firm to earn an economic profit (albeit a smaller economic profit than would exist at P^* and Q^*).

Rather than sacrifice short-term profits, an even better strategy for the incumbent firm would be to charge P^* and produce Q^*, but threaten to reduce its price to P_L and produce Q_L if a newcomer entered the market. If potential competitors are successfully deterred by such a threat, the incumbent firm could enjoy greater long-term profitability.

But the strategy is hardly foolproof. The analysis assumes the incumbent firm will produce Q_L even if a competitor enters the market. However,

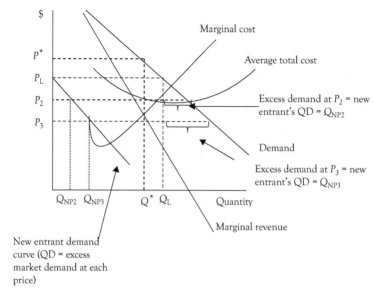

Figure 4.5 Limit pricing

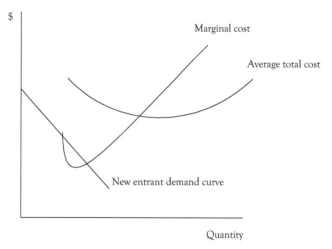

Figure 4.6 New entrant demand and cost curves under limit pricing

as noted, Q_L exceeds the firm's actual profit-maximizing output (Q^*), and the incumbent firm has an economic incentive not to make good on its threat should entry occur. If the entrant perceives these actions to be an empty threat, entry will occur anyway.

To deter entry, the incumbent firm must make the threat seem credible. One way to do this is to commit to producing Q_L units of output. By stockpiling its inventory, the firm places itself in a position in which it could easily drop its price to sell its excess production.

Limit pricing may also succeed if a learning curve exists for new entrants. Quite often, due to its experience, the incumbent firm enjoys cost efficiency advantages that newcomers will acquire over time. This implies that the average total cost curve for the newcomer is higher than that of the incumbent firm, but would eventually be identical once the firm learns how to produce more efficiently.

The analysis also assumed complete information on the part of the potential competitor. In fact, few firms know how they will fare in a new industry. A great deal of information-gathering usually takes place before a firm commits to market entry, including its breakeven output level and the funds needed to cover its losses as it penetrates the market. The lower the price charged by the existing firm, the greater the breakeven output level, and the riskier the venture to firms that aren't sure how much they can actually sell if they commit.

The incumbent firm can deter entry by virtue of its past behavior. If a large firm has established a reputation for playing hardball with new entrants in the past, it may discourage entry by a potential competitor in the future.

Even given these considerations, limit pricing may not always be the best strategy over the long run. The theory underlying limit pricing is that the firm's profits over the long-haul will be greater if it sacrifices profitability over the short term to inhibit or delay market entry. To determine whether this is really going to the case, a firm should examine limit pricing in the same manner that it would consider a capital investment. Capital budgeting determines whether a capital investment will generate an income stream that is at least as profitable as simply investing the funds at the market rate of interest. By incorporating the time value of money, the firm will move forward with the initiative only if the net present value is greater than zero.

The prospects for limit pricing can be approached in the same manner. The foregone short-term profits from limit pricing can be viewed as the equivalent of a capital investment. If the net present value of deterring market entry by way of limit pricing is greater than zero, the long-term interests of the firm are well-served by such a strategy. Otherwise, the firm is better off maximizing its immediate profits and dealing with competitors as they enter the market.

Setting up limit pricing as if it were a capital budgeting exercise may sound rather speculative, but how much more speculative is it than projecting the income stream of a capital investment over a 20-year life? Both involve some combination of data-gathering and speculation. Even if one is not predisposed toward evaluating limit pricing as an explicit net present value calculation, the firm can assume that the lower the cost of capital, the more attractive the limit pricing strategy. Or alternatively, the closer the limit-pricing profits to the profits enjoyed by a standard profit-maximizing strategy, the more attractive the limit-pricing option.

An obvious application of the viability of limit pricing involves the common practice of *price skimming*. Price skimming is often employed by firms that introduce electronic gadgets into the marketplace. The assumption is that a segment of the market is willing to pay a premium to be the first guy on the block to own the latest gadget. The firm introduces the good at a premium price with the intention of eventually lowering the price once this market segment has been thoroughly tapped. When Sony's PlayStation 3 was first introduced in the United States in 2006, for example, it was priced at $500 for its 20-GB system and $600 for its 60-GB model.[9] Six years later, a 160-GB version could be had for $249.

By employing the price skimming strategy, however, the firm runs the risk of inviting competitors into the market. An alternative strategy is to introduce the good at a lower price to slow market entry. Although the primary intent is to offer the good at a lower price in the hope of increasing market share and instilling brand loyalty, it serves the added benefit of slowing market entry.

Penetration Pricing

A *penetration pricing* strategy may allow a firm to enter a market characterized by demand-side economies of scale. To understand, consider a network to be an interconnected set of links. A *one-way network* exists when services flow in one direction, such as a waterline. One-way network can lead to a first-mover advantage because the firm enjoys cost-related economies of scale that may serve as significant market barriers. A would-be competitor must invest in expensive infrastructure to compete with the incumbent water company. The one-way network provides only supplier economies of scale because the user's value does not depend on the number of persons that use the network.

Two-way networks can be a source of demand-side economies of scale. A two-way network is similar to a phone line. The more persons who have a phone line, the greater the value of owning a phone. Other examples include instant messaging, e-mail, an airline, and so on. Consider the hub-and-spoke design of AirTran, for example. With its primary hub in Atlanta, the airline routes passengers from one of over 70 departure points through the Atlanta hub to an equal number of destinations. Hence, the Atlanta hub redistributes passengers who depart from Orlando, but who have varying final destinations.

Because the value depends on the number of users, two-way networks present significant first-mover advantage opportunities via *direct network externalities*. A phone line with only one user is worthless. A line that connects Bob and Carol has more value, and one that connects Bob and Carol and Ted has even more value. Note how the value increases with each user. If only Bob and Carol are connected, Bob can call Carol and Carol can call Bob. If Bob, Carol, and Ted are connected, Bob can call Carol or Ted, Carol can call Bob or Ted, and Ted can call Bob or Carol. A line that connects two persons allows for two connection services but a line that connects three persons allows for six.[10]

Two-way networks also give rise to *indirect network externalities*. As networks become more popular, complementary products are often developed. Instagram was developed in 2010 to allow users to take photos and share them on social networking services. Between December 2010 and April 2012, the number of users ballooned from one million to over 30 million. In April 2012, the 13-employee firm was acquired by Facebook for $1 billion in cash and stock.[11] Complementary products such as Instagram add even more to the value of the network.

Not all externalities in networks are positive. Just ask a driver along the network of highways in Los Angeles during rush hour. If usage grows to a level that cannot be served with the existing infrastructure, bottlenecking can occur.

The demand-side economies of scale can represent strong market barriers even if the new entrant offers a superior product. Suppose the first-mover is an online dating service. Because no online alternatives exist, it gathers a number of subscribers who pay $10 per month for the subscription. A second firm that offers better services is considering entering the market. Each subscriber to the first-mover recognizes that the newcomer's services are superior. However, each person also knows that the value of online dating services falls to zero if that individual switches and no one else does. The full value of the superior service is only realized if everyone switches, yet no individual has a unilateral incentive to switch. Because the first-mover advantage resulted in *consumer lock-in*, market barriers exist even for firms that offer a better service.

The penetration pricing strategy may be employed by newcomers to establish a new network. Suppose the new online dating service offers a free subscription for a limited period of time. Even though the price does not allow the new firm to recover any of its fixed costs, it places the consumer in a position of having nothing to lose by setting up an account with the new service. This allows the entrant to build its own network. If the new service is truly superior, subscribers will figure it out and eventually discard the original service.

MySpace was founded in 2003. Between 2005 and 2008, it was the most-visited social networking site in the world. By 2006, it passed Google as the most-visited website in the United States. Revenue for the social networking giant topped $900 million in 2008.[12] But hard times have fallen on the two-way network. After being overtaken by Facebook in 2009, memberships went on a steady decline, taking ad revenues down with them.[13] Recent estimates rank MySpace 161st among websites with ad revenues around $109 million.[14] Its staff dwindled from 1,400 to only 200 in three years.[15]

What went wrong? MySpace was the incumbent in the social networking market, and Facebook was the newcomer. Like MySpace, Facebook generates its revenue from advertisements, so users could set up a Facebook account at no charge. If they didn't like Facebook, they always had MySpace to fall back on. But instead of rejecting Facebook, users embraced it and began discontinuing their MySpace memberships in droves. Whereas MySpace focused on its portal strategy and entertainment content, Facebook concentrated on the social networking experience highlighted by the news feeds.

Will Facebook someday go the way of MySpace? As of this writing, Facebook was still the reigning king of social networking. But after its initial public offering in the summer of 2012, Facebook stock prices have taken a much-publicized nosedive.[16] Perhaps the much-hyped stock offering was too-hyped and overpriced. Another theory is that its user-base is shifting from the website to access via mobile devices; a shift that is much less desirable to potential advertisers. In any event, ad-revenue-based two-way networks will always be threatened by potential entrants.

Predatory Pricing

A more aggressive pricing strategy is called *predatory pricing*. Here, the incumbent firm charges a price below the marginal cost to drive a rival firm out of business. To succeed, the existing firm must have sufficient financial resources to subsidize the losses. Such a strategy could be beneficial if it deters entry by establishing a reputation for playing hardball against new entrants.

Firms considering predatory pricing have to keep several factors in mind. First, the practice violates the Sherman Antitrust Act and may violate the Robinson-Patman Act if the firm is charging different prices in differing geographical regions. Such cases, however, are hard to successfully prosecute because it isn't easy to distinguish predatory pricing from pricing to remain competitive.

Second, the predatory firm has to consider possible strategic reactions of the rival it hopes to drive out of business. When prices are set below the marginal cost, the competitor could purchase the units and stockpile them as inventory for resale when predatory pricing ends and the price rises. Similarly, any capital investment by the market entrant may be a sunk cost. Even if the incumbent firm drives the market entrant out of business, the newcomer could re-enter the market once prices rise.

Rarely is predatory pricing a viable long-term strategy for the incumbent firm. At best, a large firm with deep pockets may be able to drive a small competitor out of business, but the small firm is unlikely to serve as any real threat to the larger firm, anyway.

Product Differentiation

Product differentiation was discussed in detail in Chapter 3 as a strategy to deal with the threat of substitutes. Although product differentiation is unlikely to deter competitors from entering the market, it can help a firm withstand the effects of market entry.

This is illustrated in figures 4.7 and 4.8. Figure 4.7 shows the firm before it makes changes to its product. At the profit-maximizing price and quantity, the firm earns a normal profit.

By changing the product's attributes, the demand for the firm's good increases and becomes less elastic (because the competitors' brands become more distant substitutes). The increase in demand drives the profit-maximizing price and quantity upward. As shown in Figure 4.8, the firm enjoys an economic profit at the higher price.

Firms need to understand, however, that product differentiation only erects temporary market barriers. Any product innovation that generates an economic profit will be replicated by competing firms. Once the innovation becomes the industry standard, the firm's demand will decrease, driving profits downward toward a normal profit. Chapter 3

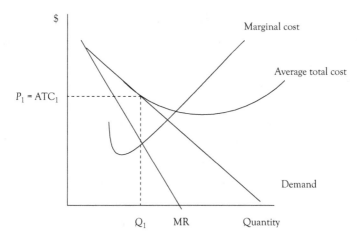

Figure 4.7 Before product differentiation

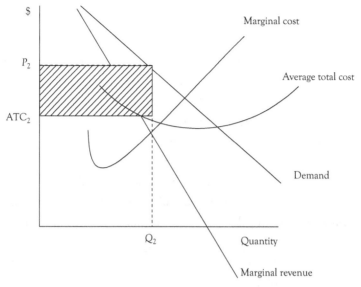

Figure 4.8 After product differentiation

reviewed the evolution of the cell phone. Each innovation intended to increase the firm's price, profits, and market share, yet the long-term effect was merely to deliver a better product to consumers at lower long-term prices.

Product innovation also comes at a cost. Firms must consider if the revenue benefits justify the costs associated with developing new product attributes.

One means of product differentiation that may also serve as a market barrier is advertising. Most pharmaceutical firms that sell over-the-counter (OTC) drugs advertise heavily even though the generic brands are bio-chemically equivalent. If firms can persuade consumers that OTC drugs with brand names are more reliable than generics, demand will increase and allow the firm to charge a higher price and enjoy greater profitability. Indeed, any visit to the local pharmacy will show fairly significant price differences between the brand name and its generic substitute. Given that many drugs were first introduced into the marketplace under the protection of a patent, advertising allows the firm to instill customer loyalty and brand identity to forestall losses in profitability once the patent expires and generics become available.

Raising Rival Firms' Costs

If rivals' marginal costs increase, they will result in decreased production which drives up prices for the dominant firms. In the U.S. Supreme Court case of *United Mine Workers v. Pennington*, the labor union allegedly conspired with the large coal operators to raise wages to drive smaller operators out of business.[17, 18] This strategy is most likely to succeed when the large-scale producers are capital-intensive whereas the smaller rival firms are labor intensive. Thus, whereas the profit margin of the large-scale operators is reduced by the higher wage rates, this is more than made up by the higher prices than can be charged in the product market. This suggests that firms that pay above the minimum wage may actually support increases in the minimum wage.[19]

If rival firms' fixed costs increase, they may deter the entry of potential competitors. Licensing is an example of a fixed cost that could deter entry. Although the incumbent firms must also pay an annual licensing fee, if the fee is high enough, it could limit the entry of rivals. California, for example, has hefty application and annual licensing fees for operating a child care center. Application fees range from $440 to $2,200, and annual fees range from $242 to $1,210.[20] In contrast, the annual licensing fees for operating a child care center in Arkansas range from $15 to $100.[21]

Price-Cost Squeezes

The price-cost squeeze is a strategy that may be initiated by a vertically integrated firm. *Vertical integration* exists when a single firm controls more than one stage of its supply chain. Later, we will discuss the strategy of vertical integration in more detail. Here, the firm drives up the costs of inputs while maintaining constant prices for the final good. The intent is to squeeze the profits of downstream competitors. As an example, the Federal Trade Commission once accused the major buyers of gasoline of overbuying crude oil to drive up its price and squeeze the profits of independent wholesalers and retailers.[22]

Summary

- Theory states that in the absence of market barriers, a firm will not be able to retain an economic profit. Firms will enter the industry and compete prices and profits downward until surviving firms have a normal profit.

- Market barriers include exclusive ownership of a key resource, supply- and demand-side economies of scale, unequal access to distribution channels, patents and copyrights, licensing, trade restrictions, and government regulations.

- Firms can delay market entry through a limit-pricing strategy. The firm sets a price that is lower than what would maximize current profits in the hope that entrants could not earn a normal profit at that price. Alternatively, the firm could charge its profit-maximizing price, but could threaten to drop its price if a firm entered the market.

- Because a limit price forces the incumbent firm to sell more output than it wants to, new competitors may enter the market anyway. Firms can signal their intent by building inventories or establishing a history of punishing newcomers.

- Limit pricing can delay the entry of firms if a learning curve exists in production. Similarly, by forcing newcomers to enter the market with lower profits, it increases the risk associated with market entry and frightens off those with risk averse preferences.

- Firms considering limit pricing should consider the long-term benefits as they would a capital budgeting decision. In general, limit pricing will be a more viable long-term strategy if interest rates are low or if the profit level associated with limit pricing is not too far from the profits enjoyed at the profit-maximizing price and output.

- Network effects can exist when there are the supply- or demand-side economies of scale. Demand-side economies of scale exist when the value of the good increases with the number of users.

- The first-mover has a significant advantage when demand-side economies of scale exist. Because the value the consumer places on the service depends on the number of users, consumer value falls if one person switches to a service offered by a new entrant, and an insufficient number of users follow suit.

- One strategy a newcomer can employ when the incumbent firm enjoys positive network effects is a penetration strategy. By offering subscriptions for free for a limited period of time, consumers can subscribe to the new service and see if they like it. If the new service is superior, they will discontinue the other one.
- Predatory pricing is when a firm sets it price below cost in an effort to drive a competitor out of business. The strategy is frequently a violation of the Sherman Antitrust Act or the Robinson-Patman Act. The strategy is not likely to succeed over the long term. If the competitor's investment in the industry is sunk, it will re-enter the market once the price rises. At best, a large firm may succeed in driving smaller firms out of business.
- Product differentiation is a way to erect temporary market barriers. A new product attribute will increase the firm's price and profit, but only until competing firms replicate the attribute. Advertising may instill brand loyalty and make the firm somewhat more resistant to market entry.
- Raising the industry's costs may also deter potential competitors from entering the industry. Higher wage rates, for example, may force small labor-intensive firms out of business, which increases the price and profits of the larger capital-intensive firms.

CHAPTER 5

Is My Supplier Holding Five Aces?

The Bargaining Power of Suppliers

A firm's profitability can be strongly influenced by the bargaining power of suppliers. Your firm may be a supplier with bargaining power. Alternatively, your firm may purchase materials from a supplier with a great deal of bargaining power. The purpose of this chapter is to outline the factors that determine supplier bargaining power.

The theory underlying gains from trade is that all transactions are mutually beneficial and that the opportunity cost of buyers and sellers drives the final price. Buyers don't have to purchase the good from a given firm; they can buy from that firm, from one of its competitors, or not at all. Buyers must recognize that firms also have choices; they can sell to a given buyer or to another buyer. And if no price is sufficient to cover costs, they may not sell at all. In general, the greater the array of alternatives to the sellers relative to those of the buyers, the greater the bargaining power of the seller.

Let's create a hypothetical scenario to illustrate the influence of the bargaining power of suppliers on prices. Suppose we have an attorney named Rick who lives alone in a small town. Rick owns his own home, and he needs to have his lawn mowed. It would normally take him an hour to mow his lawn. If he does so, he will have one less hour to put into the office work. Rick bills his clients at a rate of $150 per hour. Clearly, the opportunity cost of mowing his own lawn is $150. A 19-year-old boy named Billy lives down the street from Rick. To earn his spending money, Billy mows lawns and performs other odd jobs for neighbors. On a typical Saturday afternoon, Billy might earn an average of $10 per hour for performing such work.

To free himself to go to the office, Rick approaches Billy about mowing his lawn. Billy sizes up Rick's lawn and figures it would take him two hours. Clearly, if Billy is mowing Rick's lawn, he won't have time to perform odd jobs for any other neighbor. At a rate of $10 per hour, Billy's opportunity cost of mowing Rick's lawn is $20.

Rick and Billy must agree on a price. Billy will require at least $20. Rick, of course, is perfectly capable of mowing his own lawn, but he wants Billy to do it so he can spend his time at the office. Because he bills his clients at a rate of $150 per hour, Rick is willing to pay up to $150 to have his lawn mowed. We can reasonably assume, therefore, that Rick and Billy will agree on a price that ranges between $20 and $150.

The exact price depends on the bargaining power of Rick and Billy. Suppose Billy is the only teenager in the neighborhood. Twenty adults are seeking Billy's services. Assume all want Billy to mow their lawns so they can go to the office and bill clients at a rate of $150. Rick offers Billy $40 to mow his lawn. That's a good offer for Billy because he could only earn $20 performing odd jobs for others. But this would imply that the other adults will have to mow their own lawns. We might logically expect another adult, Paula, to offer Billy $50. In doing so, she outbids Rick while freeing herself to go to the office. In all likelihood, a bidding war will ensue, with the final price approaching $150. The key is that, whereas the entire range of prices between $20 and $150 is acceptable to all parties, the bargaining power lies primarily with Billy because he is the only seller, and 20 buyers are vying for his services.

Degree of Industry Concentration of Sellers

In this chapter, we will review the factors that determine the bargaining power of suppliers. One potential source of supplier bargaining power is the degree of industry concentration among sellers relative to buyers. In Chapter 4, we discussed the factors that might allow a single firm to dominate an industry. Monopolies can earn economic profits over the long run because market barriers keep potential competitors from entering the industry. In this chapter, we will discuss *oligopolies*, which are industries dominated by relatively few sellers. In general, *few* is usually defined as 4 to 10 firms.

Cournot Oligopoly

The key factor underlying an oligopoly is that, as the industry is highly concentrated, each firm must consider the reaction of each of its competitors when initiating a price change. Economists define various models of oligopolies. One such model is the Cournot oligopoly. In the Cournot oligopoly, few firms serve many consumers, market barriers exist, the firms may or may not sell differentiated products, and each firm makes production decisions based on the output of its competitors.

This type of oligopoly is best understood if we assume there are only two firms in the industry. Each firm determines the output that will maximize its profits, given the output produced by the rival firm. Pricing decisions bind both firms. In other words, the greater the level of output produced by the two firms, the lower the price each firm will have to charge.

The model begins with the standard assumptions of profit-maximizing price and output decisions. If only one firm is in the industry, it will enjoy monopoly power and will maximize its profits accordingly. If a rival firm produces output, the demand for the other firm's good will decrease, causing its profit-maximizing price and quantity to fall. The more output the rival firm produces, the lower the profit-maximizing price and output for its competitor. This is illustrated in Figure 5.1.

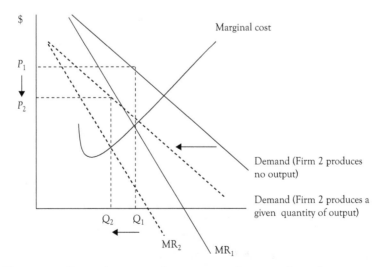

Figure 5.1 Firm 1's price and output in a Cournot oligopoly

As the graph indicates, Firm 1's profit-maximizing price (P_1) and output (Q_1) correspond to the case in which Firm 2 produces nothing. If Firm 2 produces an assumed level of output, Firm 1's demand and marginal revenue curve will shift to the left, causing its profit-maximizing price and output to fall.

The rival firm (Firm 2) is in a similar position. If Firm 1 produces nothing, Firm 2 will price and produce the profit-maximizing output that befits a monopoly. But the greater the output produced by Firm 1, the lower Firm 2's price and output.

We will refer to Figure 5.2 to help determine how the rival firms will determine their respective production levels. Firm 1's production appears along the horizontal axis whereas Firm 2's production runs along the vertical axis. We can begin by inferring that, if Firm 2 did not produce any output, Firm 1 would enjoy a monopoly and would produce its output accordingly (Q_1). If Firm 2 were to produce Q_2 units of output, the demand for Firm 1's good would decrease, causing its profit-maximizing output to fall to Q_1'. By drawing a line through the two points, we can derive Firm 1's reaction function: its profit-maximizing production levels, given the production of Firm 2.

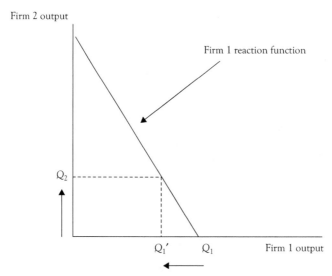

Figure 5.2 Cournot oligopoly reaction function

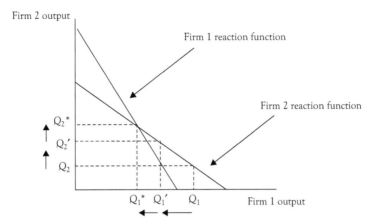

Figure 5.3 Cournot equilibrium

Figure 5.3 creates a reaction function for Firm 2 under the same set of assumptions. Firm 2 will produce its monopoly output level if Firm 1 produces nothing, but it must reduce its production as Firm 1 increases its output. Let's examine the figure to develop the ramifications for each firm's production decision. If Firm 1 produced Q_1 units of output, Firm 2 would respond by producing Q_2 units. Once Firm 2 establishes its production level at Q_2, Firm 1 will have an incentive to adjust its production to Q_1'. When Firm 1 reduces its output to Q_1', Firm 2 will change its production to Q_2'. Eventually, each firm will adjust its output until Firm 1 produces Q_1^* and Firm 2 produces Q_2^*. That the intersection of the reaction functions would represent the market equilibrium should be obvious: If Firm 1 produces Q_1^*, Firm 2 will want to produce Q_2^*, and vice versa.

What does the analysis suggest about each firm's profit? Logically, we can deduce that each firm would enjoy its maximum profit if the rival firm produced nothing. Consequently, as Firm 1 slides up its reaction function, its profits decline. The same is true for Firm 2 as it moves downward along its reaction function. Because profits are maximized for each individual firm when it enjoys a monopoly, a straight dotted line drawn to connect these output levels (Figure 5.4) shows all combinations of the firm's production that produces the same joint profit as each individual firm's monopoly profit.

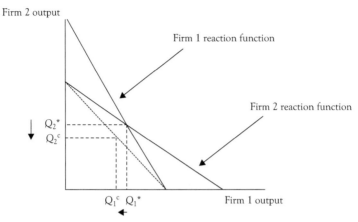

Figure 5.4 Cournot equilibrium and profits

Figure 5.4 suggests that the firms may try to benefit from collusion. According to the illustration, the two firms, agreeing to restrict their output to any combination on the dotted line (such as the combination of Q_2^c and Q_1^c) will yield combined profits equal to the profits that either would enjoy in a monopoly. In a later chapter, we will discuss collusion in more detail.

Stackelberg Oligopoly

If one firm is dominant and able to take the first-mover advantage in production decisions, a *Stackelberg oligopoly* may better characterize the outcomes. The distinction here is that the leader chooses an output level and the followers subsequently determine their own profit-maximizing output. How does the leader determine its output? Recognizing the follower's reaction function, it knows that the competitors will choose their output based on what the leader does. Consequently, the leader must determine the point along the followers' reaction functions that will maximize the leader's profit and produce the corresponding level of output.

The implications appear in Figure 5.5. Under a Cournot oligopoly, the firms would produce $Q_L^{cournot}$ and $Q_F^{cournot}$, respectively. The leader plans to take the first-mover advantage, so it determines the output along the follower's reaction function that maximizes the leader's profits. In Figure 5.4, assume that corresponds to Q_L. Given the leader's choice of output, the

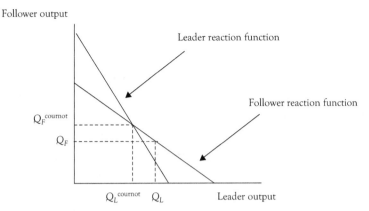

Figure 5.5 Stackelberg oligopoly

follower will produce the quantity that maximizes its own profits, or Q_F. The most notable implication is that the leader will want to produce a large quantity of output, taking a large share of the market and sizable profits. Why will the follower accommodate the leader? Why not go after the leader by producing an equally large quantity of output? According to the follower's reaction function, Q_F is the level of output that maximizes the follower's profits, given that the leader produced Q_L. Hence, any other production level will result in lower profits for the follower.

Bertrand Oligopoly

A large concentration of sellers does not guarantee more profit. The oligopoly model developed by French economist Joseph Bertand shows vigorous competition that eliminates each firm's economic profit. The *Bertrand oligopoly* shares the same characteristics as that of the other oligopolistic models in terms of a small number of firms serving a large number of consumers and the existence of market barriers. In this case, the firms are also assumed to be producing identical products with a constant marginal cost. Moreover, each firm engages in price competition and reacts to the price charged by the rival firm.

That the Bertand oligopoly leads to normal profits for each firm it should be easy to understand. As long as their products are identical, consumers will purchase from the lowest-priced firm. The result is a price war that ends when the firms charge prices that yield normal profits.

Proactive Strategies to Prevent the Bertrand Oligopoly

Building Brand Loyalty

The Bertrand model shows that rigorous price competition between two firms that produce identical products can lead to normal profits for each firm. The most straightforward tool for avoiding the *Bertrand trap* is to differentiate one's product. As noted in previous chapters, product differentiation results in less price-sensitive consumers who may become brand loyal.

The breakfast cereal industry is characterized by a high concentration of output among very few sellers. Collectively, Kellogg's, General Mills, Post, and Quaker Oats account for nearly 80 percent of the industry.[1] These firms avoid the Bertrand trap by producing a large number of brands. Kellogg's cereals range from Corn Flakes to Special K to Fruit Loops, General Mills brands include everything from Cheerios to Wheaties to Trix, Post brands include Alpha Bits, Raisin Bran, and Grape-Nuts, while Quaker Oats products range from Life to Oh!s to Puffed Wheat. Despite carrying 80 percent of the market as a group, these brands have small individual market shares. Kellogg's Corn Flakes and Cheerios tend to be the market leaders with only 5 percent of the breakfast cereal market.[2]

Beyond carrying a large number of brands, the firms vigorously advertise to distinguish the brands from the others and to instill brand loyalty. General Mills spent $869.5 million on advertising in 2014 alone.[3] Advertising-to-sales ratios average 13 percent as compared to 2 to 4 percent in other foods industries.[4] Altogether, the price—average variable cost ratio in the industry is 64 percent, far above the 26.5 percent for the aggregate food industry.[5]

Building brand loyalty is not limited to product differentiation. Most airlines offer frequent-flier programs as a way to instill loyalty. Many foods retailers offer punch cards that can earn frequent buyers a free meal.

Price Matching

Another tool to avoid the Bertrand trap is through price matching. This strategy is quite commonplace. A firm advertises that it will not be undersold and offers to match any price offered by a competitor. At first glance, this appears to be a highly competitive consumer-friendly strategy. But is it? Price wars are usually triggered by each firm's attempt to undercut the price of its competitors. But what happens if all firms in an oligopoly institute price-matching strategies? Clearly, there is no benefit to undercutting the competitor's price because the price will be instantly met. As no firm gains by undercutting prices, the price remains higher than it would have been otherwise.

Note that the price-matching strategy eliminates the need for the firm to monitor its competitor's prices. The typical strategy requires the buyer to present proof of the competitor's price, usually in the form of an advertisement. Best Buy's price-matching policy exemplifies the strategy. First, Best Buy will only match the prices of traditional brick-and-mortar competitors (i.e., no web-based prices) within a 25 mile radius of the store.[6] Second, the policy also calls for the customer to present proof of the competitor's price in the form of an ad. Best Buy reserves the right to call the competitor and confirm the price and availability of the product.

Firms seeking to employ the price-matching strategy should feel fairly comfortable that their costs of production are commensurate with the competition. If a rival firm can produce at a lower cost, it may set a price that generates a loss.

Randomized Pricing

Another strategy that can help the firm avoid the Bertrand trap is randomized pricing. Information technology makes this a viable strategy. Prior to the evolution of IT, price setting, and more importantly price changing, was a cumbersome process. Today, firms can set and reset prices quickly and easily. With online shopping, consumers can use search bots to rank the prices of specific goods from lowest to highest. This gives rival firms an opportunity to monitor the competitors' prices relatively easily and to undercut them by a slim enough margin to be the low-priced seller. If a firm changes its price relatively frequently, it becomes more difficult for rival firms to undercut one's price. Randomized pricing also makes it harder for consumers to find the low-priced vendor because its identity may change from day to day or even hour to hour.

Dependency on the Industry for Revenues

In addition to selling the products to consumers, many firms sell them to other businesses. Some firms service many industries. Theory suggests that a firm will set the price and quantity that will maximize profits from each industry it services. Suppose that a given industry represents a sizable percentage of the firm's overall revenue. In such cases, the firm may be willing to make price concessions to avoid losing industry revenues altogether. The less dependent the firm is on the industry's revenues, the more bargaining power it has over the buyer.

Buyer Switching Costs

The supplier has more bargaining power when the buyer faces high switching costs. The role of switching costs was discussed in the section on price elasticity. The higher the buyer's switching cost, the less elastic the buyer's demand curve and the less likely the buyer will switch suppliers in response to higher prices.

Faculty at many colleges and universities are familiar with the learning platform called Blackboard. Founded in 1997, the firm sought to capitalize on the movement toward Internet-based learning and online delivery. The firm patented its system in 2006 and immediately filed a patent infringement suit against its chief rival, Desire2Learn. The court battle lasted three years until the firms agreed to license each other's e-learning patent portfolios.[7]

In the meantime, existing Blackboard users have become well entrenched in the learning system. College IT personnel must be trained to use the system, and these persons must, in turn, train faculty. Aside from patent issues, switching from one provider to another would require costly retraining, making its array of current clients much less price sensitive.

Degree of Product Differentiation

A common thread to the Five Forces Model is the degree of product differentiation. The greater the distinctions between one firm's product and those of its competitors, the more inelastic the demand and the more market power afforded the suppliers.

McMenamins is a chain of over 60 brewpubs, microbreweries, music venues, historic hotels, and theater pubs in the Pacific Northwest. The common bond among its many brewhouses is that they share little in common. The company seeks out long-neglected farmhouses, movie houses, and schoolhouses, and turns them into its eclectic brand of community-based gathering places. Because each brewpub rightfully claims its uniqueness, it develops a sense of customer loyalty that makes it more resistant to prospective competitors.[8]

Lack of Substitutes

To get the best deal possible, buyers need to shop around. The fewer the number of available alternatives, the less elastic the demand, and the more leverage goes to the seller. This issue was discussed in detail in the chapter on the threat of substitutes and also in the chapter on the threat of new entrants, so there is not much need to dwell on it in this chapter. However, it's worthwhile to bring the two elements together. If a firm enjoys a monopoly with no close substitutes, the consumers' only alternative to buying from the monopolist is to do without. This makes demand more inelastic, which gives more leverage to the firm in setting a price and generating profit. This leverage is strengthened when market barriers block the potential entry of competitors.

We should also reiterate the importance of the increasing elasticity of demand over time. Because the price of a good represents opportunity cost to the buyer, consumers are always seeking ways to obtain the same or similar good at a lower price. Hence, a firm that has bargaining leverage in the short term may not continue to have such leverage over the long haul. In 1961, Ford, GM, and Chrysler combined for over 85 percent of the U.S. vehicles market.[9] The dominance of the Big Three was not lost on the United Auto Workers, which engaged in *pattern bargaining* to extract better pay and benefits for the rank and file. Pattern bargaining is the practice of targeting an employer most predisposed to a favorable contract, and then using the agreement as a precedent to demand similar collective bargaining contracts from other employers. The tactic is to remove as much price competition across employers as possible. If all employers have a similar unit cost increase, the costs can be more easily passed onto consumers in terms of higher prices.

Things began to unravel in the late 1970s when Japanese manufacturers such as Toyota, Nissan, and Honda began offering smaller, fuel-efficient cars at lower prices. Combining for roughly 0 percent of the market in 1964, these three firms had 15 percent of the market by 1980.[10] Over the long run, when the entry of auto manufacturers from abroad gave car buyers more options, the ability of the Big Three to pass along labor costs diminished. This also sapped much of the bargaining power of labor unions. In fact, union membership has been on a steady decline ever since. In 2014, union membership fell to 11.1% of the labor force, which was the lowest level in over 70 years.[11] Today, the largest producer of passenger cars is neither the United States nor Japan, but China. In 2014, China produced nearly 20 million passenger cars, whereas the United States and Japan combined for 12.5 million.[12]

Threat of Forward Integration

Most persons think of a manufacturer as a firm that sells either to wholesalers or directly to retailers. *Vertical integrated* firms are those that control both the production and distribution of the good. Forward integration occurs when the firm expands *forward* to oversee product distribution. Shell and BP, for example, control both the refineries and the distribution channels.

Vertical integration can be useful if it can reduce a firm's *transaction costs*. Consider a homeowner whose roof leaks. As this does not occur every day, the homeowner has to undergo a search for firms that can repair the leak in a timely manner. Of course, the company cannot quote a price over the phone because each job has different requirements and incurs different costs. The repair company will examine the damage and provide the homeowner with a quote. To assure the company is quoting a fair price, the homeowner must call other companies and go through the same process. All of these comprise transactions costs.

In the business world, transactions costs may be much higher if they require a specialized exchange. The buyer, for example, may require machinery that must be engineered to meet its special needs. Once the machinery has been engineered to the buyer's specifications, it has diminished value to other potential buyers. Alternatively, the relationship between the buyer and seller requires dedicated assets. A baseball field built to house a Major League Baseball team has substantially diminished value if the league does not locate a franchise there.

Note how specialized exchanges differ from most spot transactions. A consumer buying a bushel of apples from a farmer's market can quickly assess the apples made available by different farmers, compare prices, and make a selection. Transactions costs are minimal. There is no need to draw up a formal contract with the farmer or to purchase partial ownership in the farm to avoid having to shop for apples.

Specialized exchanges, on the other hand, may require costly negotiations. They may also result in underinvestment. Why would a city build a baseball field for a Major League franchise if the team could leave at any time? There is also the potential for one side to try to take advantage of the other party's sunk costs. In our baseball example, suppose the city and prospective franchise agree to build a new ballpark with 50 luxury suites. Well into the construction, the franchise suddenly demands 100 suites. In doing so, it recognizes that the city cannot undo its investment, so it is more likely to accede to the franchise's additional demands than it is to cancel the deal and allow the money spent on the facility to be squandered. Such opportunism inhibits the ability of the parties to arrive at a mutually beneficial transaction.

Contracts between the buyer and seller occur because the transactions costs are much higher if the parties attempt to engage in a spot transaction. If the supplier reengineers the product to suit the buyer's needs, the buyer must have obligations on its end. If a city agrees to build a new ballpark, the franchise must agree to occupy the space under a lease for a mutually agreed period of time. The contract also eliminates the possibility that one side will try to take advantage of the other's sunk investment. Responsibilities and liabilities are written into the contract, and any breach is actionable.

Vertical integration is an attractive option only when the transactions costs are lower than those associated with contracts. Uniting two firms as divisions of a single larger firm removes the need for contracts and eliminates the possibility that one party could take advantage of the other's sunk costs. However, vertically integrated firms incur transactions costs of their own. If the joint interests of the supplier and distributor are to be aligned, the efforts must be coordinated by a higher authority. Because the supplier's and distributor's individual interests may not be aligned with those of the joint venture, coordination may be very costly. In general, the more specific the assets in the buyer–seller relationship and the greater the potential for opportunism, the greater the costs of contracting relative to the costs of vertical integration.[13]

Many attempts to vertically integrate are based on flawed reasoning. A common rationale for integrating is to reduce volatility in earnings. However, the earnings of the manufacturer and distributor are often positively related. The same decline in demand that diminishes retailer profits will inhibit manufacturer sales.

Others argue that owning the input supply eliminates the possibility of market foreclosure, unfair prices, or supply and demand imbalances in the market for intermediate products. This may be a valid reason to integrate if one party has excessive market power. Otherwise, a firm that sets a *transfer price* that differs from the market price risks over or underproducing at the expense of profitability. For example, suppose the manufacturer (Firm B) sells its products to the retailer (Firm A). The market price at the retail end is $10 while the market price for the transfer of products from manufacturers to independent retailers is $5. If the vertically integrated firm sets its transfer price at $4 to reduce the retailer's costs, the manufacturer will only sell those units whose marginal costs are less than $4. This leaves the retailer with an inadequate inventory relative to its competitors. If the transfer price is set at $6 to increase the manufacturer's profits, the manufacturer's incentive is to overproduce relative to other manufacturers, leaving the manufacturer with excess production. In essence, economic theory asserts the following: if the marketplace at each stage of the supply chain is competitive, vertical integration will not add to the firms' collective profits.

Stuckey and White (1993) offered a litmus test for firms considering vertical integration. In general, vertical integration can be beneficial if

1. the market is too risky and unreliable;
2. companies in the adjacent stages of the supply chain have more market power than companies in your stage;
3. integration would create market barriers or allow for more effective price discrimination across market segments; and
4. the market is young and firms must integrate forward to develop a market, or, alternatively, the market is declining and independent firms are pulling out of adjacent stages.

Summary

- The greater the concentration of sellers in the industry relative to buyers, the greater the market power of the sellers.
- The Cournot oligopoly model, in which each firm determines its output in response to that chosen by its rival, demonstrates potential gains from collusion.
- In the Stackelberg oligopoly model, a dominant firm can take the first-mover advantage. The remaining firms will determine their output based on the decision of the dominant firm. Here, the dominant firm should assert its first-mover advantage by producing a large quantity of output and a dominant market share. The remaining firms will accommodate this decision because it is in their interests to do so.
- The Bertrand oligopoly, in which the firms produce identical goods and compete based on price, results in vigorous price competition that results in normal profits. This can be avoided through product differentiation, price matching, or randomized pricing.
- The seller has more market power when it is less dependent on this particular market for revenues, when buyer switching costs are high, and when there is a lack of substitutes available to buyers.

- The seller has more market power when it can threaten forward integration. Forward and backward integration rarely add to the firms' collective wealth and should be considered only when integration leads to lower transactions costs than contracting, licensing, franchising, or other alternatives to spot transactions.

- Vertical integration can be beneficial if the market is too risky and unreliable, if companies in the adjacent stages of the supply chain have more market power than companies in your stage, if integration would create market barriers or allow for more effective price discrimination across market segments, if the market is young and firms must integrate forward to develop a market, or if the market is declining and independent firms are pulling out of adjacent stages.

CHAPTER 6

When the Buyer Holds Six Aces

The Bargaining Power of Buyers

In Chapter 5, we laid out a hypothetical scenario in which Rick hoped to find someone to mow his lawn so he could go to the office. A teenager in his neighborhood, Billy, usually gets $10 per hour performing odd jobs for his neighbors. It would take him two hours to mow Rick's lawn, so if he mows Rick's lawn, he misses out on a chance to make $20 working for other neighbors. Therefore, his minimum price is $20. Rick is perfectly capable of mowing his own lawn, and could complete the task in an hour. However, he would rather have Billy do it because it will free him up to go to the office and bill clients at a rate of $150. Consequently, Rick would be willing to spend up to $150 to get his lawn mowed. Our expectation is that Rick and Billy will work out a deal and Billy will be paid somewhere between $20 and $150.

We also noted that if 20 adults like Rick were all competing for Billy's services, a bidding war would drive the price close to $150. Although the entire range of prices would have been acceptable, the bargaining power of the seller (Billy) would have driven the price to the higher end of the price range.

Let's reverse the scenario. Suppose Rick's subdivision has no less than 20 teenagers who can do a quality job of mowing his lawn, and assume that each one has an opportunity cost of $20. Let's also assume that Rick is the only person in the neighborhood whose opportunity cost of mowing his lawn exceeds $20. Hence, Rick is the only neighbor who would be willing to pay more than $20 to have his lawn mowed. In theory, if Billy offered to mow Rick's lawn for $100, Rick would be better off accepting the offer than by refusing it and mowing the lawn himself. Of course, this would imply that the other 19 teenagers would perform odd jobs for neighbors for $20. In all likelihood, one of the other teenagers, such as Eddie, would let Rick know that he would be willing to mow Rick's lawn for only $75. This would undercut Billy's price, while allowing Eddie to earn more than he could performing odd jobs for someone else. Not surprisingly, another teenager in the neighborhood, Josh, approaches Rick about mowing his lawn for $50. One could easily surmise, then, that the teens would bid the price downward until one of them mows Rick's lawn for $20. Note the result: even though the acceptable range of prices lies between $20 and $150, the bargaining power resides with the buyer (Rick) because 20 sellers are competing for a single buyer.

The purpose of this chapter is to examine the factors that influence the bargaining power of buyers. Readers should note by now that quite a bit of overlap exists between Porter's five forces. Indeed, it is the potential spillover effects of the five forces that make the model useful. A firm may be protected from new entrants to the market, but could still earn low returns if its product must contend with low-cost substitutes. Nonetheless, its returns would even be lower if market barriers were low because new entrants increase the pool of substitute goods. Thus, the collective strength of the five forces determines the ultimate profit potential of an industry.

We should note at the front end that the sources of buyer bargaining power apply both to end-use consumers and business-to-business customers. The primary difference between the two groups may lie with variations in their willingness to pay. A business purchasing an intermediate product is looking to sell it to a retailer. Because retailer prices are dictated by market forces, it is easier to quantify the acceptable price range for a wholesaler with the knowledge that the willingness to pay will not vary dramatically across wholesalers. The same is true for the retailer. In contrast, the willingness of a random person to pay for a ticket to a Beyoncé concert may vary significantly across individual consumers. Some individuals may be huge fans of the singer whereas others may not be big fans of her music and would be willing to pay very little for a ticket.

Intermediate firms may exert a strong influence on end users. Retailers determine which products will have displays, which products will sit on eye-level shelves, and which products will be pushed by their on-site staff. This link to the end user can give them quite a bit of bargaining power as they negotiate prices with suppliers. Some firms attempt to reduce the bargaining power of up- or downstream channels of the supply chain by making exclusive arrangements. Kenmore appliances, for example, are produced by a variety of manufacturers such as the Whirlpool Corporation and General Electric, but are controlled by the Sears Holdings Corporation for securitization purposes. The brand is readily identified with Sears, and now Kmart, subsequent to its acquisition by Sears in 2005.[1]

Few Buyers in the Industry Relative to the Number of Sellers

This relates to the hypothetical scenario with Rick and Billy. If Rick is the only buyer and 20 teenagers are competing to mow his lawn, he will able to get a much better price than if 20 adults were competing for a single seller.

A classic example of this type of buyer bargaining power is the defense industry. The United States Department of Defense (DOD) is the only buyer, and there are many defense contractors vying for business. As the government is the only prospective customer, contractors must compete vigorously to obtain a contract. Northrop Grumman, for example, is one of the DOD's top defense contractors and receives nearly 90 percent of its revenues from the federal government.[2]

Although one tends to think of Porter's Five Forces in terms of product markets, the same is true for labor markets. An industry for which there is one buyer of labor is called a *monopsony*. An example would be NASA in the market for astronauts. If astronauts are not hired by NASA, they must go into another profession entirely. Professional sport leagues have some level of monopsony power. Athletes seeking professional employment in the NFL, NBA, NHL, or Major League Baseball must subject themselves to a draft. Each team takes turns selecting an athlete, who must either sign with that team or sit out a year and wait for the following year's draft. Absent a draft, the most promising athletes would field offers from a number of franchises. By submitting to a draft, the club's bargaining power over the player increases tremendously. Basically, given a club offer, the player's only alternatives are to accept the offer or hold out for a better one. Once the season begins, holding out comes at a price. For this reason, most players sign well in advance of the start of the season. Although top-ranking draft picks earn quite a bit of money, their salaries would undoubtedly be even higher if they had the opportunity to shop themselves to multiple franchises.

At a lesser extreme, the average pay for radio and television announcers in 2014 was only $44,030, according to the Bureau of Labor Statistics (BLS).[3] The relatively low pay is likely a reflection of the fact that only 15,000 radio and TV stations are licensed by the Federal Communications Commission (FCC) nationwide. In fact, according to the BLS, only 30,220 persons were employed in that profession in 2014.[4] Because a large number of persons earning degrees in journalism or radio or TV are competing for so few jobs, salaries tend to be relatively low.

Degree of Product Differentiation

The theme of product differentiation arises repeatedly in the Five Forces Model. When products are undifferentiated, consumer demand is highly elastic. If competing products are virtually indistinguishable, consumers are driven by price. This results in stiff price competition that leads firms to normal profits.

The less substitutable the goods, the more inelastic the demand, and the greater the price flexibility afforded the firm. It is important to think of product differentiation as a continuum rather than as a discrete *differentiated* or *undifferentiated* choice set. Some products are fairly easy to differentiate. Post, General Mills, Kellogg's, and Quaker Oats control the majority of the ready-to-eat breakfast cereal market, but they combine for over 100 brands. Few consumers would confuse Post's Shredded Wheat with Kellogg's Cocoa Krispies. Consequently, buyers of Cocoa Krispies are less likely to substitute into Shredded Wheat if the price of Cocoa Krispies were to rise by a few cents. In sharp contrast, drivers will often bypass a service station if they know that a neighboring station is offering gas for two cents less per gallon.

Whereas it is a fairly simple task to concentrate on goods that are easy to differentiate, let's dedicate some space to an industry for which differentiation is extremely difficult: pharmaceuticals. At face value, government regulations hamstring pharmaceutical companies seeking to differentiate. The characteristics of a given drug are determined by the chemical properties of its molecule. Hence, generic drugs are biochemically equivalent to brand name drugs. Moreover, any changes in dosage, frequency, and physical characteristics must be approved by the Food and Drug Administration (FDA).

Pharmaceutical companies deal with these constraints by advertising. Promotion-to-sales ratios for prescription drugs average 10 to 20 percent, making pharmaceuticals among the most heavily promoted of all manufactured goods.[5]

At the opposite extreme, the advertising-to-sales ratio in oil refining is close to zero.[6] Oil is highly undifferentiated and marketing efforts are not likely to sway consumer perceptions.

Buyer Switching Costs

Low buyer switching costs also contribute to a more elastic demand. As an example of switching costs, the QWERTY keyboard was invented by Christopher Latham Scoles and patented in 1867. The keyboard quickly became the standard and was used to teach basic typing. Computer keyboards added various other keys (such as Page Up and Page Down), but the layout of the letters and numbers remained largely unchanged.

The QWERTY keyboard, though the industry standard, is not the only keyboard layout available and may not even be the most efficient. The Dvorak Simplified Keyboard was patented in 1936 and boasted less finger movement, higher typing rates, and fewer errors as compared with the QWERTY keyboard.[7] Although most computer operating systems allow users to convert to the Dvorak keyboard, QWERTY remains the standard. Once people have learned the QWERTY keyboard, the switching costs associated with learning the Dvorak keyboard are high.[8,9]

Buyer Threats to Integrate Backward

Backward integration occurs when distributors decide to take control of the manufacturers that supply the inputs to the final good. As reviewed in Chapter 5, economists generally take a dim view of vertical integration. When spot exchange markets are efficient, there are no gains to backward or forward integration. The primary objective in integrating backward is to reduce transactions costs. However, integrating backward incurs sizable transactions costs of its own. In general, more specific the assets in the buyer–seller relationship and the greater the potential for opportunism, the greater the costs of contracting relative to the costs of vertical integration.

Stuckey and White (1993) created a simple flowchart (Figure 6.1) to help firms that developed a new product to decide whether to vertically integrate or to pursue alternatives such as licensing or joint ventures.

As Figure 6.1 illustrates, the case for vertical integration occurs only when complementary assets that are difficult to replicate are protected by market barriers at one or more stages. Nevertheless, the Five Forces Model asserts that when opportunities for backward integration are viable, buyers who can threaten such action have more bargaining power over their suppliers.

One example of successful backward integration is Virgin Records.[10] The company began as a lone record store in 1971. The record store was barely profitable, but the firm eventually integrated backward and started its own talent management and record label. The label signed the Sex Pistols and released the album *Never Mind the Bullocks: Here's the Sex Pistols*. Over 100,000 copies of the song "God Save the Queen" were sold in the first week. But the company really struck gold when it signed Culture Club. In 1983, only 12 years after its record store was opened, the firm made a profit of $11 million, 40 percent of which came from the Culture Club.[11]

Note how the decision to integrate backward coincides with the flowchart. Records and record retailing are complementary. Each recording is unique and, therefore, impossible to legally replicate. This gives the record production company market power, making backward integration an attractive option.

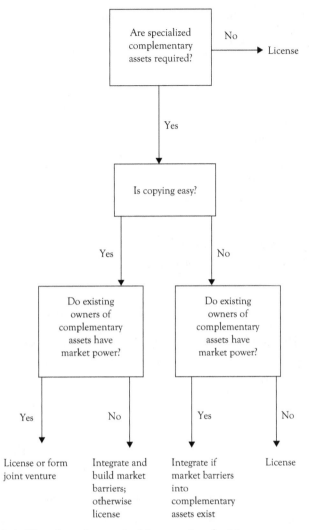

Figure 6.1 Flowchart for vertical integration decisions

Percentage of Costs Spent on Industry Purchases

If purchases within a given industry comprise a sizable percentage of the firm's overall costs, it is likely to be more price sensitive. For example, half of the cost of a convenience store is the gasoline purchased for resale. Coupled with the notion that the primary impetus for going to a convenience store is to buy gasoline, one would expect the convenience stores to be highly price sensitive when it comes to buying gas. In contrast, firms

Table 6.1 Average return on invested capital (ROIC) of selected industries, 1992–2006

Top five ROIC	ROIC (%)	Bottom five ROIC	ROIC (%)
1. Security brokers and dealers	40.9	1. Airlines	5.9
2. Soft drinks	37.8	2. Catalog, mail-order houses	5.9
3. Prepackaged software	37.8	3. Hotels	10.4
4. Pharmaceuticals	31.7	4. Knitting mills	10.5
5. Perfume, cosmetics, and toiletries	28.6	5. Soft drink bottling	11.7

whose purchases comprise a fairly small percentage of their overall costs are likely to have a more inelastic demand.

Profitability of the Buyer Group

The less the profitable the buyer group, the more elastic the demand. Firms suffering from low profit margins are more likely to be price sensitive than those boasting greater profitability. Table 6.1 shows the top and bottom five industries in terms of profitability between 1992 and 2006.[12]

The Effect of the Industry's Product on the Quality of the Buyer's Product

If the supplier's product has a strong impact on the quality of the buyer's product, the buyer is likely to have a more inelastic demand. Often, this is tied to the market segment the buyer is trying to reach. The BMW Group's mission says it all: "The BMW Group is the world's leading provider of premium products and premium services for individual mobility."[13] To fulfill its promise of premium vehicles, the firm is unlikely to cut corners if it believes doing so will jeopardize the quality of its products. At the opposite extreme, Dollar General specifically targets consumers who are focused primarily on price and are willing to trade off on quality. The focus on offering low-priced goods forces the firm to be price sensitive even if its shelves are not lined with high-quality products.[14]

The Impact of the Industry's Product on the Buyer's Other Costs

Buyers tend not to be price sensitive if the product has the potential to impact the firm's other costs. Large corporations may spend more than $500 per hour on legal services because the impact of poor legal advice can be devastating in a multimillion dollar civil suit.

Proactive Strategies to Reduce Buyer Bargaining Power

In asserting strategies to reduce buyer bargaining power, we are implicitly assuming that the firm is the seller and not a firm that is purchasing a product. Many of the characteristics that afford bargaining power to the buyer are beyond the control of the firm. However, several strategies may be implemented by the firm to limit buyer bargaining power.

Product Differentiation

Once again, product differentiation creeps into the conversation. The more standardized the product, the more consumers focus on price. Firms may differentiate their products by adding features or attributes. Sometimes advertising is all that is necessary to create brand identity and loyalty.

One factor that we have not discussed is the importance of market segmentation. In differentiating one's good, the firm has to determine its target market. Porsche and Hyundai are both automobile manufacturers, but they target entirely different market segments. Product differentiation based on market segments is one way to distance your product from competing brands.

Raising Buyer Switching Costs

This is another theme that has arisen repeatedly in this book. The lower the buyers' switching costs, the more elastic the demand. In some cases, such as sophisticated data processing systems, once the firm becomes entrenched in a system, switching costs can be very high. Some firms can create their own switching costs by offering frequent buyer programs that reward loyalty.

Exclusive Arrangements with Distributors or Retailers

Intermediate buyers can have bargaining power over producers because they have the ability to influence end users. Producers can limit this power by establishing exclusive deals with distributors or retailers, or by marketing directly to end users. DuPont, for example, advertises its STAINMASTER brand of carpet fibers to consumers as well as carpet manufacturers.

Summary

- The fewer the number of buyers in an industry relative to the number of sellers, the greater the bargaining power of the buyer. This applies to both product and labor markets.
- The more standardized the product, the greater the bargaining power of the buyer. By differentiating its goods, the buyer demand becomes less elastic and transfers more bargaining power to the seller.
- The lower the switching costs, the greater the bargaining power of the buyer. Efforts to raise buyer switching costs can shift bargaining power from the buyer to the seller.
- Backward integration is rarely advised by economists, but when the net change in transactions costs is low enough to make it a viable threat, the buyer will have more bargaining power.
- The greater the percentage of the firm's costs that is spent on industry products, the more price sensitive it will be.
- Firms with lower profit margins or returns on invested capital will be more price sensitive than firms enjoying higher returns.
- The impact of the buyer's purchase on its product quality or its other costs will be a factor in determining the buyer's price elasticity. The greater the impact on its product quality or other costs, the less price sensitive will be the firm.
- Firms can limit the bargaining power of buyers by differentiating their products, by raising consumer switching costs, by establishing exclusive arrangements with distributors or retailers, or by marketing themselves directly to consumers.

CHAPTER 7

How to Keep Firms from Beating Each Other Up

The last of the Five Forces is the degree of rivalry among competitors. Vigorous price competition pushes the industry toward normal profits. Rivalry reflects not only the intensity of competition but also the basis for competition.

Factors Influencing the Intensity of Competition

The Number of Competitors in an Industry

Economists define *perfect competition* as an industry in which many buyers and sellers coexist in a market characterized by free entry and exit, and for which the product is undifferentiated. Because so many buyers and sellers comprise the marketplace, no single buyer or seller has any bargaining power. Consequently, the basic forces of supply and demand determine the market price ($P*$), as shown in Figure 7.1.[1]

With many firms selling an undifferentiated good, consumers only care about the price. This causes each firm to face a perfectly elastic demand curve. The perfectly elastic demand curve suggests that the firm can sell as many units as it wishes as long as its price is competitive, but will sell no units at a higher price because consumers will go elsewhere. For this reason, the demand curve is horizontal and equal to the market price. Because the marginal cost of each unit is rising, the firm will produce each unit for which the price exceeds the marginal cost, but no unit for which the marginal cost exceeds the price, as shown in Figure 7.2. The profit-maximizing output for the firm is $q*$ in the illustration.

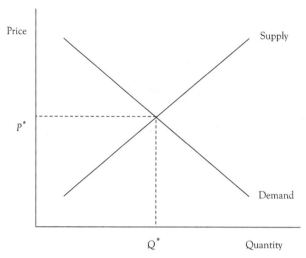

Figure 7.1 Market price in a perfectly competitive industry

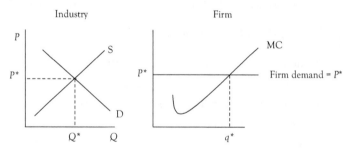

Figure 7.2 Price and output for a firm in a perfectly competitive industry

Let's add to the graph in Figure 7.2 to show the effects of free entry in a perfectly competitive market. By adding an average total cost curve, we can demonstrate that at q^*, the representative firm is earning an economic profit (i.e., at q^*, $P > $ ATC), as shown in Figure 7.3.

We can expand in Figure 7.3 to show the long-run impact of economic profits. Firms are lured into the industry by its profitability, as shown in Figure 7.4, by an increase in the industry supply. The increase in supply drives the market price downward to P_2. The individual firm must lower its price to the new market price and adjust its profit-maximizing output to q_2. At the firm's new output level, price equals the average total cost, indicating a normal profit.

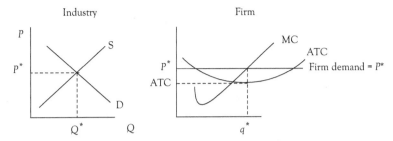

Figure 7.3 Economic profit in a perfectly competitive industry

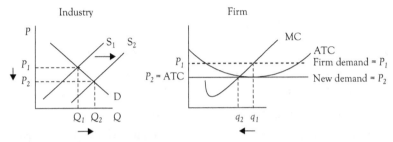

Figure 7.4 Long-run equilibrium in a perfectly competitive industry

We discussed this in detail in Chapter 4. Economic profits create an incentive for firms to enter the industry. In the absence of market barriers, economic profits will be competed away, leaving the surviving firms with a normal profit.

The perfect competition model has limited usefulness for business managers. It implicitly assumes no transportation costs (i.e., consumers are indifferent between stores at different locations) and no search costs (i.e., the time involved in shopping around for the best price). However, its basic message is important. First, the larger the number of buyers and sellers, the less bargaining power each buyer or seller has in the market. Second, the less differentiated the product, the faster the market forces will force firms toward a normal profit. Third, unless protected by market barriers or inherent cost advantages, economic profits will be competed away by entering firms.

The Speed of Industry Growth

Most managers are familiar with the product life cycle (PLC). The PLC is illustrated in Figure 7.5.

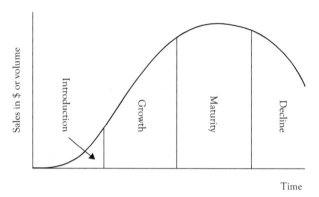

Figure 7.5 Product life cycle

When a new product is introduced (introduction stage of the PLC), unit costs are high and the product struggles to find its market. Competition is minimal because profits are low; in fact, losses are often incurred in this stage.

Economies of scale result in lower unit costs in the growth stage. Sales volume increases significantly as consumer awareness rises. Profitability increases significantly as well. This entices a few competitors to enter the industry, causing prices and economic profits to get smaller.

At the maturity stage, the market is saturated and sales volume reaches its peak. Although economies of scale continue to push unit costs downward, the industry is awash in competition. Product differentiation takes place as firms find ways to insulate themselves from the intensity of competition. Prices and profits continue to fall.

Finally, the product reaches the decline stage. Product demand decreases, causing lower prices, lower sales volume, and declining profits. Some firms begin to exit the industry.

The intensity of firm rivalry depends on where the product is currently situated in the PLC. Competition does not really begin to enter the market until the growth stage; however, rivalry is not particularly intense because the new entrants are able to establish themselves while the market is still growing. Rivalry is at its most intense in the maturity stage. Because the market is saturated, prices are falling as competitors seek to gain market share. It is here that the firms really feel the market push toward normal profits. Product differentiation begins to really take root here, as firms seek temporary barriers to slow the push toward a normal profit.

Exit Barriers

At the decline stage of the PLC, firms begin to experience economic losses. This gives them an incentive to leave the industry. However, market exit may not be easy. Earlier in this book, we created a hypothetical scenario in which Teddy was operating a Thai restaurant. Let's reproduce the income statement we created for Teddy's hypothetical Thai restaurant with one minor change. As opposed to a normal profit, Table 7.1 shows Teddy's restaurant exhibiting an economic loss. Even though the restaurant is profitable ($125,000), he could earn greater profits ($135,000) outside the restaurant business.

Table 7.1 shows that Teddy could increase his profits by $10,000 per year by getting out of the restaurant industry, but should he leave immediately? We know that if he shuts down the restaurant, he will lose $366,000 in revenue. We also know that if his restaurant shuts down, he will no longer incur $78,690 in variable costs. But what about his fixed costs? He pays $8000 per month in rent, but his lease probably calls for a penalty if he breaks it. Similar considerations may exist for equipment rental. Does he rent equipment on a month-to-month basis, or is he contractually obligated to make payments even if he no longer rents

Table 7.1 Economic loss for thai restaurant

Total revenue:		$366,000
Total variable costs:		
Meals:	$25,968	
Labor:	$52,722	$78,690
Profit contribution:		$287,310
Occupancy costs:		
Rent:	$96,000	
Equipment rental:	$11,110	
Real estate tax:	$24,000	
Personal property tax:	$6,000	
Insurance:	$18,000	
Liquor liability:	$7,200	$162,310
Accounting profit:		$125,000
Implicit cost:		$135,000
Economic profit:		($10,000)

the equipment? While considering these factors, we must distinguish between *avoidable fixed costs* and *unavoidable fixed costs*. An unavoidable fixed cost is one that will be incurred regardless of the decision being considered. Unavoidable fixed costs are sunk costs and are not relevant to the decision. Suppose, for example, that Teddy purchased a liquor license and could not resell it. The purchase price of the liquor license is an example of an unavoidable fixed cost. The fact that he paid for the license is no reason to remain with a restaurant that is less profitable than what Teddy requires to stay in business. On the other hand, suppose he is considering converting his restaurant into another style that will require redesigning. The cost of redesigning is an avoidable fixed cost. Teddy only incurs the cost if he decides to change his restaurant.

Let's go back to the income statement in Table 7.1. Let's assume all of his occupancy costs fall to zero if he shuts down his restaurant except for his rent. Suppose his lease, which runs out in six months, calls for a penalty of $25,000 if he breaks it. By breaking his lease, he will increase his income over the next 12 months by $10,000 (the amount of his economic loss), but pays a lease penalty of $25,000 for the right to do so. Hence, Teddy will be $15,000 worse off by breaking his lease. In this case, he would be better off continuing to operate the restaurant until his lease expires. On the other hand, suppose his lease calls for a penalty of $5,000. By shutting down the restaurant, his income over the next year will increase by $10,000 less the $5,000 penalty. Here, Teddy would be better off breaking the lease and getting out of the restaurant business.

Exit barriers will vary by industry and circumstance. When exit barriers are high, the firm is earning low profits and may even be losing money. Because exit is costly, a firm may remain in the industry for a longer period of time. If a firm is struggling financially, yet faces high exit barriers, we would expect that firm to engage in vigorous competition with rival firms to remain afloat.

Exit barriers are likely to be high for firms that invest heavily in capital equipment to produce a good with a very specific use. An example might be a firm that produces warships for the defense industry. In times of war, the firm invests heavily to supply the nation's defense needs. During peacetime, the demand for specialized warships decreases. If the avoidable fixed costs associated with retooling are prohibitively high, the firm may remain in business even though it loses money.

Commitment to the Industry

Economic theory suggests that economic losses should cause firms to leave an industry, but that doesn't always happen. Some CEOs and top-level managers have so much of their lives personally invested in the company that they will be the last on the ship if it sinks; they believe they have the ability to turn things around when times get tough.

The Bertrand oligopoly was discussed in detail in Chapter 5. In that model, price wars could arise that would drive firms toward normal profits, even if there are very few firms in the industry. Imagine an industry with a relatively inelastic market demand curve. If the major competitors became obsessed with increasing market share, a price war could cause revenues and profits to fall.

Poor decisions may not always be linked to stubbornness. Economists frequently talk about *principal-agent issues* in corporations. Although the goal of a firm is to maximize profits, the goal of individual employees is to maximize self-interest. Left alone, many employees would show up late for work, leave early, take long lunches, and spend time at work posting on Facebook and texting friends. Expense accounts would yield more extravagant tastes, and higher level management would acquire a taste for the good life in terms of company cars and country club memberships—all paid for by the company.

The solution is to align compensation with performance and to create an organizational structure that allows for behavior to be monitored. Sales personnel are rewarded for closing deals. They report to a branch manager who is rewarded for the performance of the branch. The branch manager reports to a regional sales manager who is rewarded for the performance of the region, and so on. At the highest level, top-level managers answer to the stockholders. In this manner, each supervisor has a vested interest in assuring those who report to him are behaving in a manner consistent with the goals of the firm.

Firms often create reward systems in the form of rank-order tournaments.[2] As the namesake implies, they operate in much the same way as professional tennis tournaments. A pro tennis tournament is set up like a pyramid. The winners from the first round progress to the second round, and the winners from the second round progress to the third round. Each round entitles the victors to more prize money. Eventually, one of the players becomes the champion and receives the greatest prize money.

Many businesses have a similar structure. Promotions are rewarded with significant increases in salaries and benefits. The pyramid nature of the organization guarantees that not every aspiring manager will be promoted; hence, the rewards go to the highest producers.

Nonetheless, incentive structures to align performance with rewards sometimes fail, not because the reward is insufficient to motivate the employees, but because the employee may be able to manipulate the firm to earn rewards at the expense of the best interests of the firm. The Enron scandal of the early 2000s is perhaps the most notorious example of a misalignment of performance and rewards. Corporate management was heavily rewarded with stock options. At face value, this would appear to align rewards with corporate goals. If managerial decisions were consistent with the long-term health of Enron, stock prices would rise. Instead, it led to a myopic focus on short-term stock prices. In 1999, the stock soared by 56 percent and increased by an additional 87 percent the following year.[3] By using accounting loopholes, special purpose entities, and poor financial reporting, the firm was able to hide billions of dollars in debt. In one year, fears of impending bankruptcy caused the stock price to plummet from $90 per share to less than $1 per share. Enron filed for bankruptcy in late 2001.

The $218 million bonus payments that accompanied the bailout of the American International Group, Inc. (AIG) in 2009 sparked a national outrage. A bubble in the housing market led to the proliferation of subprime mortgages that were packaged into mortgage-backed securities and sold to investors. When the housing bubble burst, Congress approved the troubled asset relief program (TARP) that included a $700 billion bailout in an effort to stave off a financial meltdown that might have led to another Great Depression. AIG, which received $170 billion in bailout funds, spent $218 million on bonuses. Although these were defended as *retention bonuses,* payments necessary to retain knowledgeable persons who could disentangle the mess, 52 of the persons receiving bonuses had, in fact, already left the firm.[4]

Whether a product of poorly designed reward structures or myopic perspectives on the value of competition, some firms are prone to losing focus on the long-term goals of the company when making decisions. This can lead to Bertrand-like outcomes even if relatively few competitors exist in the industry.

Familiarity with Rival Firms

Basic oligopoly models such as the Cournot, Stackelberg, and Bertrand models are based on reaction functions. Unlike the perfect competition model, in which no firm is large enough to have much of an influence on the overall market, oligopolies are characterized by a relatively small number of firms that collectively control a large share of the market. The reaction functions described in Chapter 5 are based on the notion that firms anticipate their competitors' reactions before initiating a pricing strategy. The automobile industry, for example, is well known for its low annual percentage rates (APRs) and rebate programs in the late summer or early fall. The intent is to clear out inventory to make room for the following year's models. Ford is well aware that if it introduces zero percent APR on new car purchases, its competitors will likely follow suit based on the past experience. If firms lack experience in dealing with each other, they may misinterpret each other's strategies. This could result in intense price competition that erodes economic profits rather quickly.

The Cournot oligopoly model introduced the notion that firms could benefit by colluding to restrict production to boost prices and profits. Price fixing is a practice deemed illegal by the Sherman Antitrust Act of 1890. Nonetheless, firms are occasionally accused of conspiring to fix prices. In 2009, for example, several manufacturers of LCD panels were accused of price fixing in sales of LCD panels in televisions, notebook computers, and monitors. Samsung, Sharp, and five other manufacturers paid a combined $553 million in settlement damages.[5]

Economic theory suggests that collusion is unlikely to succeed except in special circumstances. To understand why, we will rely on *game theory*. The matrix in Figure 7.6 is based on the assumption that there are two

Firm Y

Firm X		Low price	High price
	Low price	Low profit, low profit	Highest profit, lowest profit
	High price	Lowest profit, highest profit	High profit, high profit

Figure 7.6 Matrix of profits under each pair of prices

firms in the industry: Firm X and Firm Y. Each firm must decide whether to charge a high price or a low price. We will assume they are producing an undifferentiated product such that buyers will purchase from the low-price firm. As such, if prices differ, the low-priced firm will enjoy its greatest profit, and the high-priced firm will incur its lowest profit. If the prices are the same, both firms will enjoy greater profits at the higher prices.

The first number in each cell indicates Firm X's profit under each scenario. For example, if Firm X charges a low price and Firm Y charges a high price, Firm X will enjoy its highest profit. On the other hand, if Firm X charges a high price and Firm Y charges a low price, Firm X will earn its lowest profit. The second number in each cell represents Firm Y's profit under each pair of prices. They reveal a similar pattern regarding Y's profits: specifically, Y profits the most when it undercuts X and earns the smallest profit when X charges a lower price than Y.

Note also the results when both firms charge the same price. Both X and Y are better off when both charge high prices than when they both charge low prices.

Game theory analyzes strategy by determining the best action of one firm given the strategy adopted by the other. According to the matrix, if Firm Y charges a low price, Firm X should charge a low price because it is better off with a low profit than with its lowest profit. If Firm Y charges a high price, Firm X will want to charge a low price because it would rather earn its highest profit than just a high profit. Note that regardless of what Firm Y does, Firm X is always better off charging a low price. Because a single strategy (charging a low price) is best for Firm X regardless of what Firm Y does, we say that Firm X has a *dominant strategy* to charge a low price.

A quick glance at the matrix will reveal that Firm Y also has a dominant strategy to charge a low price. The logic of the matrix should be apparent. If one firm charges a high price, the other firm profits by undercutting its competitor's price. If the rival firm charges a low price, the firm is better off matching the price than allowing it to be undercut.

Note that if both firms charge a low price, they both will earn a low profit. Will one of the firms raise its price in the hope that the other one will follow suit? As the matrix indicates, if Firm X raises its price, Firm Y will enjoy its highest profit. Why would Firm Y raise its price and allow its profit to fall? This means that Firm X, by raising its price, will earn its lowest profit. The same will hold true if Firm Y raises its price. Firm X, by keeping its price low, will reap its highest profit, so its profits will fall if it increases its price. This implies that if Firm Y raises its price, its profits will fall to their lowest level. The notion that neither side can unilaterally change its strategy and be better off is called a *Nash equilibrium*.

This particular variation of game theory, called the *prisoner's dilemma*, is interesting. Note that at the Nash equilibrium, both firms exhibit low profits. Yet if both firms were to agree to raise their prices, they would both enjoy high profits. Earlier, we noted the potential gains from collusion while discussing the Cournot oligopoly. The matrix in Figure 7.6 indicates similar gains to colluding.

But successful collusion is much more difficult in practice. Recall that each firm has a dominant strategy to charge a low price. If each firm agrees to charge a high price, both firms will enjoy high profits. But if one of the firms defects from the agreement and charges a low price, it will earn its highest profit. Although both firms gain from colluding, each firm has an incentive to cheat on the agreement by lowering its price. Moreover, both firms recognize the other's incentive to cheat.

How can the firms enter into a collusive agreement without fear of cheating? Let's begin with a *one-shot game*. Firms X and Y agree to raise prices and then simultaneously reveal a price. Firm X knows that if Firm Y raises its price, Firm X can reap its highest profit by charging a lower price in violation of the agreement. Equally important is X's recognition that Y has the same incentive: To play Firm X for a sucker and to undercut its price for its own maximum gain. Hence, each firm could charge a low price either as an aggressive strategy to take advantage of the opponent or as a defensive strategy because the firm fears the opponent cannot be trusted. Game theory suggests that the Nash equilibrium will win out in

Firm Y

Firm X		Low price	High price
	Low price	$0, $0	$15, ($5)
	High price	($5), $15	$10, $10

Figure 7.7 Matrix of profits under each pair of prices

the one-shot game. Sticking with your end of the agreement is a gamble, but charging a low price is the safest bet.

But what if the firms play the game repeatedly? Let's replace the cells with actual numbers to show how collusion can succeed, as shown in Figure 7.7.

According to the matrix, neither firm will profit if they both charge a low price. (It's best to think of this scenario as where each firm earns a normal profit). Both firms can earn economic profits by colluding.

We can also see the individual gains that can be achieved by cheating. If the firms collude, each firm can earn $10. If one of them cheats, the cheater's profits rise to $15 while the other firm incurs a loss of $5.

For the sake of argument, assume that the firms successfully collude in the *first round* of the game and each firm earns a $10 profit. In round 2, Firm X decides to cheat. In doing so, its profits rise to $15. Thus, by violating the agreement, Firm X's profits increased by $5. But what about round 3? By establishing itself as a cheater, under no circumstance will Firm Y agree to collude in the future. Firm X cannot be trusted, so Firm Y will charge a low price in round 3. Firm X, knowing that Firm Y will not charge a high price, has no choice but to also charge a low price. In round 3, therefore, Firm X will earn $0 profit.

If we tabulate the profits through three rounds, we will see why Firm X may not want to cheat. By cheating in round 2 and having the Nash equilibrium prevail in round 3, X's profits total $25 through the three rounds. But suppose it hadn't cheated in the second round? By sticking to the collusive agreement, Firm X could have earned profits totaling $30. By defecting to increase its profits in round 2, it wound up being $5 worse off after three rounds.

Economists refer to this as *infinitely repeated games*. The critical element is this: by defecting in a given round to raise its profits, the rival firm will punish the cheater in future rounds. Firm X may have increased its profit in round 2 by $5, but its profits in round 3 were $10 less than what could have been earned in that round had X not cheated. Hence, its collective profits over three rounds declined by $5. This is why the Nash equilibrium will prevail in the one-shot game. The only consideration that might keep a firm from cheating on a collusive agreement is the fear of future punishment that will more than wipe out anything gained by defecting. But in the one-shot game, there can be no future punishment. Therefore, in the one-shot game, collusion cannot succeed.[6]

One should note that the infinitely-repeated game should represent the norm for most industries. After all, prices are set and reset almost continually. If firms agree to collude and one of them lowers its price, the rival firm can lower its price to punish the cheater. The gains from cheating may not be wiped out immediately, but eventually, any gains from cheating will be eroded by competitive pricing. Does this mean that collusion is potentially foolproof? Hardly. Throughout this book, we noted that in the absence of market barriers, economic profits will attract new firms to the industry. If a handful of firms can successfully collude to generate economic profits, it is only a matter of time before new firms are lured into the industry. The increase in market supply cannot sustain the high prices, causing the firms to abandon the collusive strategy and compete prices downward.

Factors Influencing the Basis of Competition

In addition to the intensity of firm rivalry, there are various dimensions that form the basis for competition. When firms begin to compete on the same dimension, such as price, profitability will suffer. We will discuss various factors that are often associated with vigorous price competition.

Undifferentiated Products and Low Switching Costs

This theme has arisen repeatedly throughout this book. The more standardized the product and the easier for consumers to switch firms, the more likely price competition will erode profits. As noted in earlier chapters, some products are easier to differentiate than others. Milk from dairy farms often carries the dairy's name, but consumers cannot distinguish one dairy's milk from another. Not surprisingly, then, the advertising-to-sales ratio for dairy products is relatively low at 2.9 percent.[7]

Even when relatively little difference exists between competing products, firms can sometimes find ways to differentiate. Hotels have a hard time differentiating themselves. Although hotels often promote themselves as budget hotels or as *4-star* hotels, it isn't particularly easy for one 4-star hotel to distinguish itself from another 4-star hotel. Credit cards are even more standardized. What makes a Visa purchase any more or less desirable than a MasterCard purchase?

This is when cobranding can help both interests. The Hilton— American Express card allows cardholders special benefits when staying at Hilton hotels. This gives the consumer an incentive to stay at Hilton hotels and to use the card on visits. Service stations cobrand with fast-food restaurants for the same reason. Absent the adjoining restaurant, the service station offers a standardized product. But cobranding with McDonald's or Subway creates distance between that service station and the nearest competitor.

Firms also avoid price competition by raising switching costs. Flights are even harder for consumers to distinguish than hotel rooms. Most consumers select their flights on the basis of price, departure or arrival times, and number of connections. Most airlines offer frequent-flier programs to raise consumer switching costs.

Degree of Operating Leverage

Operating leverage refers to a firm's fixed costs as a percentage of its total costs. The higher the percentage of fixed costs relative to total costs, the more leveraged the firm. One should note that both the airline (5.9 percent) and hotel industry (10.4 percent) rank near the bottom of the list of industries in terms of return on invested capital.[8] Both industries are highly leveraged. The marginal cost of a seat on a plane or a hotel room is negligible. Consequently, firms in both industries compete vigorously to fill their seats or rooms.

Let's examine the impact of operating leverage on unit sales and profitability. Assume Firm A has fixed costs of $1,250 and variable costs of $20 per unit. Firm B is more leveraged: its fixed costs are $5,000, with variable costs of $5 per unit. For simplicity's sake, assume the current

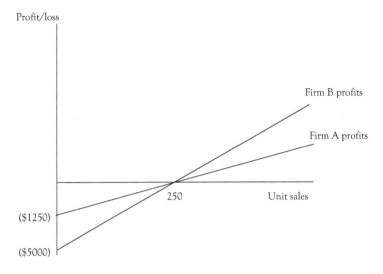

Figure 7.8 Degree of operating leverage

price charged by both firms is $25. The cost and price figures have been rigged to allow the breakeven quantity to be identical for both firms at 250 units.

Figure 7.8 shows the ramifications for profitability at each output level. If unit sales are equal to zero for both firms, Firm A's losses total $1,250 whereas the more leveraged firm's losses are equal to $5,000. As the figure shows, at all levels of unit sales prior to the breakeven point, the more leveraged firm posts greater losses. Once the breakeven level has past, the leveraged firm enjoys greater profits.

Since the airline industry was deregulated in 1978, airlines have relied extensively on *price discrimination* to make their profits. Price discrimination is the practice of charging different prices to different customers based on their willingness to pay.[9] Sophisticated software such as SABRE is combined with pricing policies to allow the airline to charge higher prices to business travelers while keeping prices low to fill remaining seats with leisure travelers. When a new entrant enters the market for a given route, market pressures reduce the ability of airlines to charge higher prices to travelers with the greatest willingness to pay.[10]

The pressure to cut prices can be particularly intense in an economic downturn. For less leveraged firms, a decline in demand implies a decrease not only in revenues but also in variable costs. Profits will likely decline

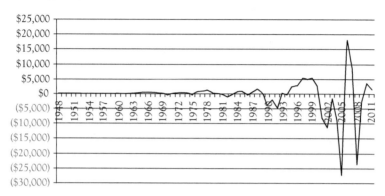

Figure 7.9 *Net income in the airline industry by year (in millions of dollars)*

in hard times, but the decreased variable costs will shelter the firm from imminent disaster. For more leveraged firms, decreases in variable costs are relatively small because most of the firm's costs are composed of fixed costs. Because their fixed costs must be paid, and marginal costs are low, firms can resort to price wars that virtually guarantee they will suffer a loss. Indeed, research shows that troughs in the business cycle reduce price dispersion among competing carriers.[11]

Consistent with Figure 7.9, the airline industry has been characterized by extreme fluctuations in profitability since deregulation in 1978.[12] As Figure 7.9 indicates, profits were fairly stable until deregulation. Since that time, the industry has been subject to extreme fluctuations in profits, with losses spiking when the economy is weak, such as in 2008.

Ability to Expand Capacity

Although we've discussed the price elasticity of demand in great detail, we have not examined the *price elasticity of supply*, which refers to the responsiveness of producers to price changes. A firm's ability to respond to price changes is limited by its capacity. Assume a firm has a capacity of 10,000 units. At the current price of $50, suppose it maximizes its profits by producing 8,000 units. Assume the price doubles and the firm determines it would maximize its profits by increasing production to 15,000 units. Unfortunately, due to its capacity constraints, the firm can

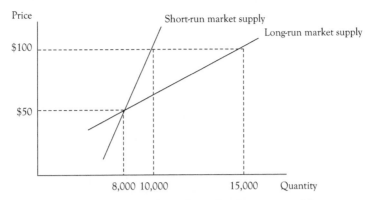

Figure 7.10 Price elasticity of supply in the short run and long run

only increase production to 10,000 units, as shown in Figure 7.10. As the graph indicates, the capacity constraint causes the firm's supply curve (short-run market supply) to be relatively inelastic.

The firm's profits are constrained by its limited capacity. It wants to produce 15,000, but is limited to 10,000 units. In time, it builds a second 10,000-unit-capacity facility so it can increase production to 15,000 units. Note that this causes the firm's supply curve to become more elastic. One should also note that the increase in capacity is not a shift in the supply curve. If the price were to go back to $50, the firm would want to return to 8,000 units.

However, overcapacity creates pressures to cut prices. To illustrate, let's make some changes in Figure 7.10. First, we'll change the firm's supply curve to an industry supply curve. Second, we'll add a demand curve to show how the interaction of supply and demand determines the market price. Figure 7.11 shows the results. Because the firms have capacity constraints, an increase in demand causes the market price to rise from $50 to $100. Industry production rises from Q_1 to Q_2.

In time, firms respond to the profit incentive by increasing capacity. This results in excess production at $100 ($Q_3 - Q_2$), causing firms to compete prices down to $70, with industry production falling from Q_3 to Q_4.

Given this model, one should not be surprised that Phoenix, Arizona, was among the cities hardest hit when the housing bubble burst. According to estimates, Phoenix ranked third among U.S. cities in terms

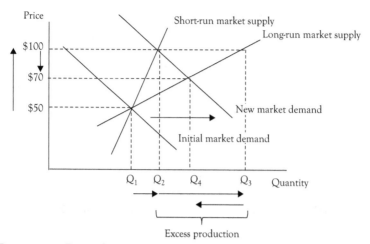

Figure 7.11 *Price elasticity of supply and the response to overcapacity*

of housing supply elasticity.[13] Not surprisingly, then, when the subprime mortgage crisis hit, median Phoenix housing prices plummeted from a peak of $268,000 in June 2006 to only $121,000 in February 2009.[14]

Perishability of the Product

For most firms, unsold inventory can be stored and sold at a later date. If the product is perishable, firms have no little choice but to slash prices to dump excess inventory. An example that might come to mind is produce at the supermarket or baked goods. If they go unsold for a modest period of time, they will rot or begin to mold. Hence, the firm is better off lowering the price even if it causes the firm to lose money than throwing the goods away.

Examples of perishable products are not limited to foods. Seats on a plane are perishable to the extent that once a plane leaves the ground an unsold seat is foregone revenue. It cannot be *stored* and sold another day. Because the marginal cost of an empty seat is so low, the airline is better off selling the seat at a price near the marginal cost than for the plane to take off with an empty seat. The same goes for hotel rooms. A room that goes empty for an evening is a room that could have generated revenue. As with the seat on the plane, because the marginal cost of a night at a hotel room is so low, the hotel is better off renting the room at a low price than allowing it to go unused for the night.

Other goods that can be perishable are clothing and computer equipment. Computers evolve so rapidly that they can become obsolete rather quickly. Much clothing is seasonal in nature. Storing it for the following season is not only costly, but risky because some clothing styles change from year to year.

Summary

- The greater the number of firms in the industry, the more intense the level of firm rivalry and the faster profits will be competed toward the normal profit level.
- When industry growth is slow, firm rivalry will be more intense. This is likely to occur at the maturity stage of the product life cycle.
- When exit barriers are high, firms may remain in the industry and compete vigorously. Exit barriers will be higher when avoidable fixed costs are high.
- Firm rivalry will be high when rivals are committed to the industry. This may be associated with principal-agent problems in which high-level managers are rewarded for the short-term performances of their firm.
- Rivalry will be greater when firms are less familiar with each other. Attempts to collude with rival firms are rarely successful because each firm has an incentive to violate its agreement. Only when each firm stands to be punished by rivals for cheating can collusion succeed. Even this will enjoy limited success if the colluding firms are not protected by market barriers.
- When products are undifferentiated and switching costs are low, price competition can be intense. This can be alleviated by raising switching costs, differentiating one's good, or through cobranding.
- When operating leverage is such that fixed costs are high and variable costs are low, there exists a potential for strong price competition.

- The price elasticity of supply becomes more elastic over time as firms are better able to adjust their capacities. This creates the potential for overcapacity to lead to intense price competition.
- When goods are perishable and cannot be stored for future sale, price competition may be intense. Certain foods, seats on planes, and hotel rooms are examples of perishable goods.

Appendix I

How Strong Is Your Firm's Competitive Advantage? Summary of Factors and Strategies

Force that affects profitability	Factors affecting that force	Proactive strategies
Threat of substitutes	1. price/performance of substitute 2. buyer switching costs	1. product differentiation 2. raising buyer switching costs 3. tying
Threat of new entrants	1. supply-side economies of scale 2. demand-side economies of scale 3. buyer switching costs 4. capital requirements 5. incumbent firm advantages 6. access to distribution channels 7. government policy 8. expected retaliation	1. limit pricing 2. penetration pricing 3. product differentiation 4. raising rival firms' costs 5. price-cost squeezes
Bargaining power of suppliers	1. degree of industry concentration of sellers 2. dependency on the industry for revenues 3. buyer switching costs 4. degree of product differentiation 5. availability of substitutes 6. threat of forward integration	1. building brand loyalty 2. price matching 3. randomized pricing 4. product differentiation
Bargaining power of buyers	1. number of buyers in the industry relative to the number of sellers 2. degree of product differentiation 3. buyer switching costs 4. buyer threats to integrate backward 5. percentage of costs spent on industry purchases 6. profitability of the buyer group 7. effect of the industry's product on the quality of the buyer's product 8. impact of the industry's product on the buyer's other costs	1. product differentiation 2. raising buyer switching costs 3. exclusive arrangements with distributors or retailers

(Continued)

(*Continued*)

Force that affects profitability	Factors affecting that force	Proactive strategies
Rivalry among existing firms	1. number of competitors in the industry 2. speed of industry growth 3. exit barriers 4. commitment to the industry 5. familiarity with rival firms 6. degree of product differentiation 7. buyer switching costs 8. degree of operating leverage 9. ability to expand capacity 10. perishability of the product	1. product differentiation 2. raising buyer switching costs 3. cobranding

Appendix II

Relevant Published Case Studies

Available through Harvard Business Publishing.

1. Borders Group, Inc.
2. Netflix, Inc.: Streaming Away from DVDs
3. Movie Rental Business: Blockbuster, Netflix, and Redbox
4. Swimming in the Virtual Community Pool with Plenty of Fish
5. MySpace
6. Virgin Group: Finding New Avenues for Growth
7. The Fall of Enron
8. Google, Inc.
9. *The New York Times* Paywall
10. eReading: Amazon's Kindle
11. Forever: De Beers and U.S. Antitrust Law
12. Price-Fixing Vignettes
13. Bitter Competition: *The Holland Sweetener Co. vs. NutraSweet*
14. Viagra in China: A Prolonged Battle over Intellectual Property Rights
15. The Huffington Post
16. Reed Supermarkets: A New Wave of Competitors
17. The Hawaiian Airline Industry, 2001–2008
18. Zoltek
19. Sony Ericsson: Marketing the Next Music Phone
20. Bling Nation
21. Entrepreneurs at Twitter: Building a Brand, a Social Tool or a Tech Power-house?
22. Branding Yoga
23. Design Thinking and Innovation at Apple
24. Rapid Rewards at Southwest Airlines
25. Bally Total Fitness
26. Wii Encore
27. Emerging Nokia
28. Keurig: From David to Goliath: The Challenge of Gaining and Maintaining Marketplace Leadership
29. Uber: 21st Century Technology Confronts 20th Century Regulation

Notes

Chapter 1

1. Gregorowicz and Hegji (1998).
2. For a more thorough critique of the managerial economics curriculum, see Marburger (2011).

Chapter 2

1. As the firm expands its capacity, some of these factors will vary with output.
2. We are going to set aside the obvious conflict of interest that the teens might prefer to take their time so as to increase their individual earnings. Suppose the objective was to pay for a trip to Hawaii.
3. Many persons who have had a course in microeconomics may recall the rule that a firm maximizes its profits at the output level where MR = MC. In fact, this is the graphical representation of a firm that produces every unit for which MR > MC and no unit where MC > MR.
4. Porter (1979).

Chapter 3

1. The opportunity cost of the consumer's time is also relevant to purchase decisions. If the consumer got an offer from A and then traveled to B and got the same offer, then he would probably buy the car from dealership B. To keep the analysis simple, we will assume that if the price is the same for identical vehicles, the consumer will be indifferent to both of them.
2. Trachtenberg and Fowler (2009).
3. Amazon (2011).
4. Barnes & Noble (2012).
5. Anderson (2009), Bhatt (2010), Minzeheimer (2011).
6. Welsh (2011).
7. Peoples (2009).
8. Friedlander (2014).
9. Wasserman (2012).
10. White, Kapoor, and Dumais (2010).
11. White, Kapoor, and Dumais (2010).

12. Guo, White, Zhang, Anderson, and Dumais (2011).
13. http://gs.statcounter.com
14. http://gs.statcounter.com
15. The Evolution of Cell Phone Design (2009); Walters (2011).
16. Koo, Koh, and Nam (2004).
17. Zimmerman (2012).
18. For more on the economics of tying and its legality, see Marburger (2012).

Chapter 4

1. Coase (1979).
2. Marburger and Marburger (2009).
3. Maynard (2012).
4. Wong (2013).
5. Maurizi (1974), Leland (1979).
6. Simon (2011).
7. Lubin (2010).
8. This would normally result in lower profits because the marginal cost exceeds the marginal revenue for all units in excess of Q*.
9. *USA Today* (2006).
10. If the number of users is n, the number of potential connection services is n(n–1).
11. Primack (2012).
12. Arrington (2011).
13. Chmielewski and Sarno (2009).
14. Arrington (2011).
15. Vascellaro, Steel, and Adams (2011).
16. Krantz (2012).
17. Williamson (1968).
18. Salop and Scheffman (1983).
19. As evidenced in Lerner (2009).
20. http://ccld.ca.gov/res/pdf/AllFeesCCP.pdf
21. http://humanservices.arkansas.gov/dccece/licensing_docs/2014%20A1%20CCC%20Clean%20Copy%20Final%20Filing.pdf
22. Scheffman and Higgins (2003).

Chapter 5

1. Nevo (2001).
2. Nevo (2001).

3. General Mills (2011).

4. Nevo (2001).

5. Nevo (2001).

6. Best Buy (2012).

7 Blackboard (2009).

8 Tichgelaar (2012).

9. Wall's Auto (2012).

10. Wall's Auto (2012).

11. Bureau of Labor Statistics (2014).

12. International Organization of Motor Vehicle Manufacturers (2012).

13. Klein, Crawford, and Alchian (1978).

Chapter 6

1. Berner (2007).

2. Northrop Grumman (2011).

3. Bureau of Labor Statistics (2014).

4. Bureau of Labor Statistics (2014).

5. King (2000).

6. Advertising Age (2014).

7. Liebowitz and Margolis (1990) challenge the widely-held notion that the Dvorak keyboard is superior to the QWERTY keyboard.

8. Diamond (1997).

9. My international travels to countries such as Germany and Belgium have allowed me to experience the switching costs associated with a different keyboard. They are not insignificant.

10. Buchanan (2010).

11. Virgin Records (2012).

12. Porter (2008).

13. BMW Group (2015).

14. McClatchy Newspapers (2012).

Chapter 7

1. We haven't discussed the law of supply, which asserts that the higher the price, the greater the quantity produced. At any given price, every unit that can be sold for a profit (i.e., for which the price exceeds the marginal cost of the unit) will be produced. Because marginal costs are rising, the higher the price, the more units can be sold at a profit. Hence, the market supply curve is upward sloping.

2. Lazear and Rosen (1981).
3. Healy and Palepu (2003).
4. *Countdown with Keith Olbermann* (2009).
5. Freifeld (2011).
6. Economists also describe the finitely repeated game. Real-world examples of finitely repeated games are rare, so the discussion here will be brief. In short, if the number of rounds is finite and known to both sides, there is no fear of punishment in the final round. Therefore, the Nash equilibrium will prevail. But since the result of the final round is predetermined, the next-to-the-last round cannot be met with future punishment (i.e., the rival firm will punish you no matter what you do). If we follow this through to the first round, game theory predicts that the Nash equilibrium will prevail at every round; hence, collusion cannot succeed in the finitely-repeated game.
7. Advertising Age (2012).
8. Porter (2008).
9. For an extensive analysis of price discrimination strategies, see Marburger (2012).
10. Gerardi and Shapiro (2009). However, this empirical finding is not universal (Stavins, 2001).
11. Gerardi and Shapiro (2009).
12. Figures taken from Airlines for America at www.airlines.org
13. Green et al. (2005).
14. Goldman (2009).

References

Advertising Age. 2014. "Advertising to Sales Ratio by Industry." Advertising Age. http://adage.com/article/datacenter-advertising-spending/advertising-sales-ratios-industry/106575/ (accessed June 12, 2015).

Anderson, M. 2009. "Borders Plans to Sell E-Books." Huffington Post. http://www.huffingtonpost.com/2009/12/16/borders -plans-to-sell-ebo_n_394072 .html (accessed April 19, 2012).

Arkansas Department of Human Services. 2014. http://humanservices.arkansas. gov/dccece/licensing_docs/2014%20A1%20CCC%20Clean%20Copy%20 Final%20Filing.pdf (accessed August 13, 2015).

Arrington, M. 2011. "Exclusive: The Bleak Financial Numbers from the Myspace Sale Pitch Book." Tech Crunch. http://techcrunch.com/2011/04/12/ exclusive-the-bleak-financial-numbers-from-the-myspace-sale-pitch-book/ (accessed August 8, 2012).

Barnes & Noble. 2012. http://www.barnesandnobleinc.com/our_company/our_ company.html (accessed April 19, 2012).

Bell, D. 2008. "Best iPod-Compatible Alternatives." CNET. http://reviews.cnet. com/8301-12519_7-10104294-49.html (accessed May 22, 2012).

Berner, R. 2007. *The New Alchemy at Sears*. Bloomberg Business Week. http://www.businessweek.com/stories/2007-04-15/the-new-alchemy-at-sears (accessed July 3, 2012).

Best Buy. 2012. http://www.bestbuy.com/site/Payment-Pricing/Best-Buy-Price-Match-Guarantee/pcmcat204400050011.c?id=pcmcat204400050011 (accessed June 11, 2012).

Bhatt, N. 2010. "Borders to Sell Kobo E-Book Reader for $199." IT News. http://www.itnews.com.au/News/174625,borders-to-sell-kobo-e-book-reader-for-199.aspx (Accessed April 19, 2012).

Blackboard, Desire2Learn Announce Patent Cross License Agreement. 2009. Desire2Learn. http://www.desire2learn.com/news/newsdetails_154.php (Accessed June 20, 2012).

BMW Group. 2015. "Corporate Facts. Corporate Strategy." BMW Group. http://www.bmwgroup.com/bmwgroup_prod/e/0_0_www_bmwgroup_ com/investor_relations/fakten_zum_unternehmen/strategie.html (accessed June 12, 2015).

Buchanan, R. 2010. "Examples of Vertically Integrated Companies." Chron.com. http://smallbusiness.chron.com/examples-vertically-integrated-companies-12868.html (accessed July 2, 2012).

Bureau of Labor Statistics. 2014. "News Release." http://www.bls.gov/news. release/pdf/union2.pdf (accessed June 11, 2015).

Bureau of Labor Statistics. 2014. "National Occupational Employment and Wage Estimates United States." http://www.bls.gov/oes/current/oes273011. htm (accessed June 12, 2015).

California Department of Social Services. 2012. Community Care Licensing Division. http://ccld.ca.gov/res/pdf/AllFeesCCP.pdf (accessed October 30, 2012).

Chmielewski, D., and D. Sarno. 2009. "How MySpace Fell Off the Pace." *L.A. Times.* http://articles.latimes.com/2009/jun/17/business/fi-ct-myspace17 (accessed August 8, 2012).

Coase, R. 1979. "Payola in Radio and Television Broadcasting." *Journal of Law and Economics* 22, no. 2, pp. 269–328.

Countdown with Keith Olbermann for Wednesday, March 18. 2009. MSNBC. http://www.msnbc.msn.com/id/29773574/ (accessed July 5, 2012).

Crist, R. 2014. "Keurig 2.0 Brews up DRM to Freeze out Copycat Cups." CNET. http://www.cnet.com/news/keurig-2-0-brews-up-drm-to-freeze-out-copycat-cups/ (accessed June 9, 2015).

Diamandis, P. 2014. "Uber Versus the Law (My Money's on Uber)." Forbes. www.forbes.com/sites/peterdiamandis/2014/09/08/uber-vs-the-law-my-moneys-on-uber/ (accessed June 5, 2015).

Diamond, J. 1997. "The Curse of QWERTY." *Discover Magazine.* http:// discovermagazine.com/1997/apr/thecurseofqwerty1099/article_view?b_ start:int=0&-C= (accessed July 2, 2012).

Eldon, E. 2014. "D.C. City Council "Uber Amendment" Would Force Sedans to Charge 5x Minimum Taxi Prices." TechCrunch. http://techcrunch. com/2012/07/09/dc-city-councils-uber-amendment-would-force-sedans-to-charge-5x-taxi-prices-and-kill-uberx/ (accessed June 5, 2015).

Friedlander, J. 2014. "News and Notes on 2014 RIAA Music Industry Shipment and Revenue Statistics." RIAA. http://riaa.com/media/D1F4E3E8-D3E0-FCEE-BB55-FD8B35BC8785.pdf (accessed May 29, 2015).

Freifeld, K. 2011. "LCD Price-fi Xing Suit Results in $553 Million Settlement." Huffington Post. http://www.huffingtonpost.com/2011/12/27/lcd-price-fi xing-settlement_n_1171313.html (accessed July 10, 2012).

Gara, T. 2012. "The K-Cup Patent is Dead. Long Live the K-Cup." *The Wall Street Journal.* http://blogs.wsj.com/corporate-intelligence/2012/11/28/the-k-cup-patent-is-dead-long-live-the-k-cup/ (accessed June 9, 2015).

General Mills 2014 Annual Report. 2014. General Mills. http://www. generalmills.com/en/Company/Overview (accessed June 11, 2015).

Gerardi, K., and A. Shapiro. 2009. "Does Competition Reduce Price Dispersion? New Evidence from the Airline Industry." *Journal of Political Economy* 117, no. 1, pp. 1–37.

Goldman, R. 2009. "As Home Prices Fall, Phoenix Housing Market Rises from Ashes." *ABC News.* http://abcnews.go.com/Business/story?id=7619908 &page=1 (accessed July 6, 2012).

Green, R., S. Malpezzi, and S. Mayo. 2005. "Metropolitan-Specific Estimates of the Price Elasticity Supply of Housing and Their Sources." *American Economic Review Papers and Proceedings* 95, no. 2, pp. 334–339.

Gregorowicz, P., and C. Hegji. 1998. "Economics in the MBA Curriculum: Some Preliminary Survey Results." *Journal of Economic Education* 29, no. 1, pp. 81–87.

Guo, Q., R. White, Y. Zhang, B. Anderson, and S. Dumais. 2011. "Why Searchers Switch: Understanding and Predicting Engine Switching Rationales." Microsoft. http://research.microsoft.com/en-us/um/people/ sdumais/sigir2011-searchengineswitching-fp348-guo.pdf (accessed August 8, 2012).

Healy, P., and K. Palepu, 2003. "The Fall of Enron." *Journal of Economic Perspectives* 17, no. 2, pp. 3–26.

International Organization of Motor Vehicle Manufacturers. 2014. "Production Statistics." OICA. http://www.oica.net/category/production-statistics/ (accessed June 11, 2015).

King, C. 2000. "*Marketing, Product Differentiation, and Competition in the Market for Antiulcer Drugs.* Harvard Business Publishing. http://hbswk.hbs. edu/archive/1850.html (accessed July 2, 2012).

Klein, B., R. Crawford, and A. Alchian. 1978. "Vertical Integration, Appropriable Rents, and the Competitive Contracting Process." *Journal of Law and Economics* 21, no. 2, pp. 297–326.

Koo C., C. Koh, and K. Nam. 2004. "An Examination of Porter's Competitive Strategies in Electronic Virtual Markets: A Comparison of Two On-Line Business Models." *International Journal of Electronic Commerce* 9, no. 1, pp. 163–180.

Kosner, A. 2014. "Beats Music Acquisition Gives Apple a Way Out of the iTunes and Apps Store Traps." Forbes. http://www.forbes.com/sites/ anthonykosner/2014/05/29/beats-music-acquisition-gives-apple-a-way-out-of-the-itunes-and-app-store-traps/ (accessed May 29, 2015).

Krantz, M. 2012. "Four Reasons Investors Don't "Like" Facebook and How to Fix It." *USA Today.* http://www.usatoday.com/money/perfi/stocks/ story/2012-08-01/facebook-stock-woes/56658246/1?csp=34money (accessed August 8, 2012).

Lazear, E., and S. Rosen. 1981. "Rank-Order Tournaments as Optimum Labor Contracts."*Journal of Political Economy* 89, no. 5, pp. 841–864.

Leland, H. 1979. "Quacks, Lemons, and Licensing: A Theory of Minimum Quality Standards." *Journal of Political Economy* 87, no. 6, pp. 1328–46.

Lerner, D. 2009. "Business Owners Welcome Minimum Wage Increase." Business for a Fair Minimum Wage. http://www.businessforafairminimumwage.org/node/89 (accessed July 8, 2012).

Liebowitz, S., and S. Margolis. 1990. "The Fable of the Keys." *Journal of Law and Economics* 33, no. 1, pp. 1–25.

Lubin, G. 2010. "*25 American Products That Rely on Huge Protective Tariffs to Survive*." Business Insider. http://www.businessinsider.com/americas-biggest-tariffs-2010-9# (accessed May 31, 2012).

Magretta, J. 1998. "The Power of Virtual Integration: An Interview with Dell Computer's Michael Dell." *Harvard Business Review* 76, no. 2, pp. 72–84.

Marburger, D. 2012. *Innovative Pricing Strategies to Increase Profits*. New York: Business Expert Press.

Marburger, D.L., and D.R. Marburger. 2009. "The Free Ride That's Killing the News Business." *LA Times*. http://articles.latimes.com/2009/aug/02/opinion/oe-marburger2 (accessed May 31, 2012).

Marburger, D.R. 2011. "Re-Designing Managerial Economics to Suit the MBA." *International Journal of Pluralism and Economics Education* 2, no. 2, pp. 196–205.

Maurizi, A. 1974. "Occupational Licensing and the Public Interest." *Journal of Political Economy* 82, no. 2, pp. 399–413.

Maynard, M. 2012. "What New Orleans Can Expect When Its Newspaper Goes Away." Forbes. http://www.forbes.com/sites/michelinemaynard/2012/05/24/what-new-orleans-can-expect-when-its-newspaper-goes-away/2/ (accessed from).

Minzeheimer, B. 2011. "Is There Hope for Small Bookstores in a Digital Age." *USA Today*. http://www.usatoday.com/life/books/news/2011-02-10-1Abookstores10_CV_N.htm (accessed April 19, 2012).

Nevo, A. 2001. "Measuring Market Power in the Ready-to-Eat Cereal Industry." *Econometrica* 69, no. 2, pp. 307–42.

Northrop Grumman 2014 Annual Report. 2014. Northrop Grumman. http://www.northropgrumman.com/AboutUs/AnnualReports/Documents/pdfs/2014_noc_ar.pdf (accessed August 21, 2015).

Peoples, G. 2009. "iTunes Price Change Hurt Some Rankings." Billboard. http://www.billboard.com/biz/articles/news/1272039/itunes-price-changes-hurt-some-rankings (accessed, May 22, 2012).

Porter, M. 1979. "How Competitive Forces Shape Strategy." *Harvard Business Review* 57, no. 2, pp. 137–45.

Porter, M. 2008. "The Five Competitive Forces that Shape Strategy." *Harvard Business Review* 86, no. 1, pp. 78–93.

Primack, P. 2012. *"Breaking: Facebook Buying Instagram for $1 Billion." CNN Money.* http://finance.fortune.cnn.com/2012/04/09/breaking-facebook-buying-instagram-for-1-billion/?section=magazines_fortune (accessed June 3, 2012).

Salop, S., and C. Scheffman. 1983. "Raising Rivals' Costs." *American Economic Review Papers and Proceedings* 73, no. 2, pp. 267–71.

Scheffman, C., and R. Higgins. 2003. "Twenty Years of Raising Rivals' Costs: History, Assessment, and Future." *George Mason Law Review* 12, no. 2, pp. 371–87.

Simon, S. 2011. "A License to Shampoo: Jobs Needing State Approval Rise." *The Wall Street Journal.* http://online.wsj.com/article/SB1000142405274870344 5904576118030935929752.html (accessed May 31, 2012).

USA Today. 2006. "Sony's PS3 Makes U.S. Debut to Long Lines, Short Supplies." http://www.usatoday.com/tech/gaming/2006-11-17-ps3-debut_x.htm (accessed June 1, 2012).

StatCounter Global Stats. 2012. Statcounter. http://gs.statcounter.com (accessed October 30, 2012).

Stavins, J. 2001. "Price Discrimination in the Airline Market: The Effect of Market Concentration." *Review of Economics and Statistics* 83, no. 1, pp. 200–02.

Stein, B. 2001. "The DeBeers Story: A New Cut on an Old Monopoly: The Company That Has Ruled Diamonds for a Century Wants to Polish Its Image and Dominate as Never before." CNN. http://money.cnn.com/magazines/fortune/fortune_archive/2001/02/19/296863/index.htm (accessed May 30, 2012).

Stuckey, J., and D. White. 1993. "When and When Not to Vertically Integrate." *MIT Sloan Management Review* 34, no. 3, pp. 71–83.

The Evolution of Cell Phone Design (1983–2009). 2009. Web Designer Depot. http://www.webdesignerdepot.com/2009/05/the-evolution-of-cell-phone-design-between-1983-2009/ (accessed May 27, 2012).

Tichgelaar, J. 2012. Preserved in Alcohol: Case Studies of Adaptive Reuse Projects by McMenamins, Inc. Arkansas State University Heritage Studies.

Trachtenberg, J., and G. Fowler. 2009. "B&N Reader out Tuesday." *The Wall Street Journal.* http://online.wsj.com/article/SB10001424052748703816204 574483790552304348.html (accessed April 19, 2012).

Vascellaro, J., E. Steel, and R. Adams. 2011. "News Corp Sells MySpace for a Song." *The Wall Street Journal.* http://online.wsj.com/article/SB100014240 5270230458400457641593227377 0852.html (accessed August 8, 2012).

Virgin Records. 2012. "Virgin Records 1972–1983." Virgin. http://www.virgin.com/history/virgin-records-1972-1983 (accessed July 2, 2012).

Wall's Auto. 2012. "U.S.Vehicles Sales Market Share by Company, 1961–2011." Wall's Auto. http://wardsauto.com/keydata/historical/UsaSa28summary (accessed June 29, 2012).

Walters, R. 2011. "Inforgraphic Shows Evolution of the Cell Phone." Geek. http://www.geek.com/articles/mobile/infographic-shows-evolution-of-the-cell-phone-20111018/ (accessed May 27, 2012).

Wasserman, T. 2012. "Bing Overtakes Yahoo as Number Two Search Engine." Yahoo! News. http://news.yahoo.com/bing-overtakes-yahoo-number-two-search-engine-study-152511416.html (accessed August 7, 2012).

Welsh, J. 2011. "Hybrid Sales Surge as Gas Prices March Upward." *The Wall Street Journal.* http://blogs.wsj.com/drivers-seat/2011/04/06/hybrid-sales-surge-as-gas-prices-march-upward (accessed October 31, 2012).

White, R., A. Kapoor, and S. Dumais. 2010. "Modeling Long-Term Search Engine Usage." Microsoft. http://research.microsoft.com/en-us/um/people/sdumais/UMAP2010-LongTermSwitching.pdf (accessed August 9, 2012).

Wong, V. 2013. "Rival K-Cup makers are climbing Green Mountain." Bloomberg. http://www.bloomberg.com/bw/articles/2013-08-09/rival-k-cup-makers-are-climbing-green-mountain (accessed August 21, 2015).

Williamson, O. 1968. "Wage Rates as a Barrier to Entry: The Pennington Case in Perspective." *Quarterly Journal of Economics* 82, no. 1, pp. 85–116.

Zimmerman, A. 2012. "Showdown Over Showrooming." *The Wall Street Journal.* http://online.wsj.com/article/SB10001424052970204624204577177242516227440.html (accessed August 8, 2012).

Index

OTHER TITLES FROM THE ECONOMICS COLLECTION

Philip Romero, The University of Oregon and
Jeffrey Edwards, North Carolina A&T State University, Editors

- *Fiscal Policy within the IS-LM Framework* by Shahdad Naghshpour
- *Monetary Policy within the IS-LM Framework* by Shahdad Naghshpour
- *Building Better Econometric Models Using Cross Section and Panel Data* by Jeffrey A. Edwards
- *Basel III Liquidity Regulation and Its Implications* by Mark Petersen
- *Saving American Manufacturing: The Fight for Jobs, Opportunity, and National Security* by William R. Killingsworth
- *What Hedge Funds Really Do: An Introduction to Portfolio Management* by Philip J. Romero and Tucker Balch
- *Advanced Economies and Emerging Markets: Prospects for Globalization* by Marcus Goncalves, Jose Alves, and Harry Xia
- *Comparing Emerging and Advanced Markets: Current Trends and Challenges* by Marcus Goncalves and Harry Xia
- *Learning Basic Macroeconomics: A Policy Perspective from Different Schools of Thought* by Hal W. Snarr
- *The Basics of Foreign Exchange Markets: A Monetary Systems Approach* by William D. Gerdes
- *Learning Macroeconomic Principles Using MAPLE* by Hal W. Snarr
- *Macroeconomics: Integrating Theory, Policy and Practice for a New Era* by David G. Tuerck
- *Emerging and Frontier Markets: The New Frontline for Global Trade* by Marcus Goncalves and Jose Alves
- *Doing Business in Emerging Markets: Roadmap for Success* by Marcus Goncalves, Jose Alves, and Rajabahadur V. Arcot
- *The Foundations of Economic Theory* by Fred Foldvary
- *The Market Economy* by Fred Foldvary
- *Economic Theory in Practice* by A.P. O'Malley
- *Community Economics* by Emmanuel A. Frenkel
- *Seeing the Future: How to Build Basic Forecasting Models* by Tam Bang Vu
- *U.S. Politics and the American Macroeconomy* by Gerald T. Fox
- *Global Public Health Policies: Case Studies from India on Planning and Implementation* by KV Ramani
- *Innovative Pricing Strategies to Increase Profits, Second Edition* by Daniel Marburger

Announcing the Business Expert Press Digital Library

Concise e-books business students need for classroom and research

This book can also be purchased in an e-book collection by your library as

- a one-time purchase,
- that is owned forever,
- allows for simultaneous readers,
- has no restrictions on printing, and
- can be downloaded as PDFs from within the library community.

Our digital library collections are a great solution to beat the rising cost of textbooks. E-books can be loaded into their course management systems or onto students' e-book readers.
The **Business Expert Press** digital libraries are very affordable, with no obligation to buy in future years. For more information, please visit **www.businessexpertpress.com/librarians**. To set up a trial in the United States, please email **sales@businessexpertpress.com**.